A FRESH START

- Four fishermen who worked endless hours for uncertain wages.
- An invalid who had almost given up hope of walking again.
- A mechanic whose work is filled with customer complaints.
- A middle-aged couple who used to go to church—but haven't been there lately.
- You. Me.

What do we all have in common? The need for a fresh start. These daily devotional readings on the Gospel of John can help renew, rebuild, and refresh each of us in our spiritual walk.

A Fresh Start

A devotional study
of the Gospel of John

Steve Harper

David C. Cook Publishing Co.
ELGIN, ILLINOIS—WESTON, ONTARIO

A FRESH START
© 1979 David C. Cook Publishing Co.
All rights reserved. Except for brief excerpts for review
purposes, no part of this book may be reproduced without written
permission from the publisher.

Scripture quotations are from the New International Version.

Published by David C. Cook Publishing Co., Elgin, IL 60120
Cover design and photo by Rich Nickel
Printed in the United States of America

ISBN 0-89191-188-X
LC 79-51744

To Jeannie, John, and Katrina
God's greatest gifts to me

PREFACE

The Gospel of John has been a source of inspiration throughout the history of Christianity. New Christians are often counseled to begin their Bible study in this book. Older Christians find it a good place to go for new discoveries. Regardless of where we are in the faith when we read John, it speaks.

This series of daily readings is for anyone who wants to make a fresh start. Perhaps you are a new Christian beginning a whole new way of life. Or you may be a Christian who feels this is a time when God would have you rededicate yourself to him. Maybe you come to this book in the midst of a pilgrimage in which God is challenging you with many new experiences. I trust that wherever you are, you will find a helpful message in these pages.

As a pastor I am keenly aware of the need to place resources in people's hands that will motivate them to grow in their faith. I am often asked to recommend resources for spiritual growth. Also, I know that there is a great need in the church today to stress the life of discipleship. We must begin to talk in terms of a Christian *life-style,* and that is precisely what discipleship is. Through these meditations I want to share with you the many ways our discipleship can be expressed in daily living.

These messages have grown out of my own quiet times with God. They have developed in response to real-life situations I have faced. They are not ivory-tower speculations about the faith; they are firsthand experiences as a result of living it. The readings are intentionally short so you can make them part of your daily spiritual nourishment, and so you will be stimulated to do more thinking on your own. The pages that follow this introduction give the rationale for structuring each meditation as I have.

Over the next three months I hope several things will happen in your life. First, I hope you will grow in your faith and in your understanding of discipleship. Second, I hope you will discover the Gospel of John in a new way. Third, I hope you will discover a method of encountering God daily that will strengthen you in your faith. One of the joys of writing a book like this is in knowing that it is possible to study any book in the Bible in the same way.

If we could visit over a cup of coffee I would urge you to begin this pilgrimage with your notebook beside you. Record your own impressions. Make your own applications. Write your own prayers. Let this book lead you to your own personal discoveries. God's Word is food for our spirits; we need to feast on it as we do on our daily bread. My prayer as you begin this adventure is that God will feed you richly in the days ahead!

I want to express personal thanks to my secretary, Margaret Burns, and my wife, Jeannie, for typing the manuscript. I also want to thank the members of Wesley United Methodist Church in Borger, Texas, who encouraged me and prayed for me in the final days of writing.

How to Use This Book to the Greatest Advantage

The format of this book is intended to help you grow in your faith. Each daily reading follows a similar pattern, and each part of that pattern is meant to accomplish a purpose.

First, notice the *general Scripture reading*. By reading these passages each day, you will go through the entire Gospel in three months. This will expose you to the book's total message, but there is another reason why these readings are important. They will give you the overall context from which the devotion is taken, and you will need to see the whole before you look at a part.

Second, there is the *specific text*. This is usually a verse or phrase that struck me as I read devotionally through the Gospel. If you were writing a book, you might have chosen another one. In fact, your spiritual notebook is a good place to write down the specific messages you receive. The text I have selected is one that I believe will aid you in your daily walk and strengthen you in your discipleship.

Third, there is *the devotion*. Again, this is my personal response to the text—what God has taught me. You may see something else; you may see more. The daily reading is not meant to tie all the ends together so much as it is meant to stimulate your thinking. The devotional readings are not a theological commentary but are life-centered. I hope during the next three months you will cultivate the ability of going to the Word of God and reading it in such a way that it will touch your life. There are other ways to read the Bible (e. g., exegetically), but every disciple must learn to read the Word for daily impact.

Fourth, there is *the prayer*. You will notice that the prayers are short. They are not meant to be your prayer, although you may pray them as written. Rather, they are meant to be suggestive and helpful for you in making your own prayer for the day.

I hope that after three months you will have developed a lifelong pattern of having a regular devotional time that will affect your daily living and help you maintain vital communication with your heavenly Father.

BELIEVE AND LIVE

Scripture: John 20:30-31

Text: *These are written that you may believe that Jesus is the Christ, the Son of God, and that by believing you may have life in his name (v. 31).*

If you could sit down with John and ask him why he wrote this Gospel, his answer would likely be similar to the verse you have just read. And before you get into the material itself, it is always good to know why it is written. We are fortunate that John puts into words his motivation for writing under the inspiration of the Holy Spirit. This verse serves as a window through which we can view the entire book; it is a door that swings open, inviting us to enter.

John is not writing to pass on information or to preserve facts. He is writing so that something may happen to those who read his words. He wants all who read to come to belief and life.

Can it be that there is an inseparable relationship between one's belief and one's life? John thinks so. God thinks so, for as a man "thinks in his heart, so is he" (Prov. 23:7, Amplified). Right now, in large measure, you are what you believe.

There is something powerful here. Belief in Jesus gives life. But what is belief? Just saying, "I believe"? No, belief for the Christian includes trusting in, relying on, and clinging to Jesus. That is the kind of belief that gives life.

When I go out on the lake I wear a life preserver. By trusting in it, relying on it, and clinging to it, I can know that my life is safe. We can know a new dimension of life awaits us if we believe in Jesus. All that John writes is for the purpose of helping us believe and live!

Dear God, all this time I thought I was living. Can it be there is a difference between being alive and really living? Can it be that to really live I must believe—that belief and life go together—that belief in Jesus is the way to life? John thinks so. God, help me to find out. Use this Gospel to show me. I give you my life. Teach me. And help me follow what you show me. Amen.

THE GOOD WORD

Scripture: John 1:1-5

Text: *In the beginning was the Word (v. 1).*

My wife, Jeannie, was a cheerleader in high school. One of the yells they did was "What's the good word?" For every game there was a good word.

Does God have a good word for life? John says, "Yes! The good word is Jesus." As we begin our devotions in this Gospel, let us see what John has to say in these opening verses about Jesus, the Word:

1. He is eternal; he existed from the beginning.
2. He is with God; he is separate in person from the Father.
3. He is God; he is one in nature with the Father.
4. He is the agent of creation; he brought all things into being.
5. He is life; no one really lives without him.
6. He is light; he illumines and guides our lives moment by moment.
7. He is power; nothing can overpower him.

Admittedly, this is a deep truth. But because it is deep, it is beautiful. The depths of life are covered by Jesus—God's good Word. No experience can be had of which he is not a part. No question can be asked that he cannot answer. No situation is too tough for him to handle.

Someone has said that Jesus is the best photograph of God. To know him is to know God. To see him is to see the Father. What's the good Word for your life? *Jesus!* Why? "The Word became flesh and lived for a while among us" (John 1:14). God became a man. Because that's so, God can handle any problem we may have. He's been there. He is here now. That's the good word.

Heavenly Father, in the midst of all the bad words I hear and feel, I really need your good Word. Thank you for coming to me in the person of Jesus. Because you took on human life, you understand what I am going through. And you have come to me in a way I can understand. Thank you for wanting me to hear your good Word. Amen.

GOD'S FORERUNNER

Scripture: John 1:6-9

Text: *There came a man who was sent from God; his name was John (v. 6).*

God could not drop Jesus into Palestine. The people were not ready. There had been no prophetic word in Israel for four hundred years. Preparation was necessary.

So God sent John the Baptist as his forerunner. He came to "prepare the way for the Lord" (Mark 1:3). God used him to get things ready so that Christ and the gospel could make their penetration.

God can't drop Jesus into your heart or mine either. We are not ready. We can't handle it. So God sends many different forerunners to get us ready.

I shared this idea with a men's group one morning and asked them to tell what forerunners God had used to get them to the place where the gospel could be heard and Christ received. Without exception, every man had one or more things to share. The list was interesting: books, sermons, special pastors, friends, parents, Sunday school teachers, mates, etc. Each of these had become someone's "John the Baptist."

What is your "John the Baptist"? What has God used as a forerunner in your life to open you to the gospel of Jesus Christ? Have you realized that without these things you probably would have never become a Christian?

Now one more question. Do you know that God may well use you as someone else's John the Baptist? That's a sobering thought, but is it exciting! Today God may just use you to "prepare the way for the Lord" for another!

God, thank you for those "John the Baptists" in my life that prepared my heart for faith in you. Somehow, Lord, help them to know how grateful I am. Let me so live among others today that I may be someone's forerunner too. Amen.

THE ULTIMATE INVITATION

Scripture: John 1:10-13

Text: *Yet to all who received him, to those who believed in his name, he gave the right to become the children of God (v. 12).*

My children delight in receiving invitations. They know something special is going to happen, something that will be fun and exciting. Even as an adult I like to get invitations and take part in the events.

In this verse we have God's ultimate invitation. It is the invitation to become a personal participant in the exciting event of salvation. In the middle of describing his Word, God says that you and I can be related to him and his children.

John is careful to spell out exactly how that happens. He says that we become children of God by *receiving* the Word, Jesus Christ, for ourselves. And the act of receiving is related to the word *believe*. We receive Jesus into our lives by believing in his name.

Believing involves more than just accepting Christ with our minds. It means that we so identify ourselves with Jesus that we are willing to trust him completely, follow him exclusively, and serve him faithfully all the rest of our lives. To truly believe in Jesus means that we respond to God's invitation by giving him our lives.

That's not really so unusual. Every invitation I have received had the letters *R.S.V.P.* on the bottom, indicating that the sender wants to know if I plan to be a part of the event. The same is true of God's offer of salvation. He has sent this wonderful invitation to everyone, but as he does he asks for a response.

Today you have read God's ultimate invitation. Have you made your response? If you have, then you can show your commitment by the way you live this day. If you have not, there is no better time than right now to receive him, believe in his name, and become his child.

Heavenly Father, thank you for this invitation to personally participate in your great salvation. I accept your invitation with thanksgiving, and I confirm my acceptance by giving you my life. In Jesus' name. Amen.

THE GREAT FACT

Scripture: John 1:14

Text: *The Word became flesh, and lived for a while among us (v. 14)*.

E. Stanley Jones is one of the world's best-known missionaries. For most of his life he labored in India, seeking to win men and women to Jesus Christ. And in his ministry he used this verse over and over to point out the uniqueness of Christianity. For "Brother Stanley," as he was affectionately called, this was one of the most important verses in the Bible.

The uniqueness lies in the fact that the Word that John has been describing did not remain a word. The Word became a person! E. Stanley Jones used to say that in other world religions the Word remains word. Ideas remain ideas. Philosophies remain philosophies. But in Christianity, the Word becomes *flesh*. God actually visits this planet in the person of his Son, Jesus. And that is unique. In other religions the call is "Reach up to God if you can." In Christianity the call is "God has reached down to us."

God in Jesus Christ has experienced life just like you and I live it. He understands our frustrations, temptations, and failures. He knows what it is like to feel pressure and loneliness. The God who made us is the God who understands us.

This also means that God our Creator has come to show us the "way out." The existentialist Jean-Paul Sartre once wrote that life had no exit. But the Gospel of Jesus Christ says life has an exit. And it not only has an exit, it has a *hope.* In coming to this world God has put his blessing on life and declared it worth living. And by coming into this world he has given us the example of abundant living as well as the power to live abundantly.

This is the great fact of life. Search the world over, and you will not find anything greater to give your life to. Look anywhere you please, and you will never find a better reason for living. God has come to us *personally* in Jesus. And because of that, life has the potential of being marvelously new!

Dear God, thank you for giving me new life in Christ. As I live today, I will meet people who may feel trapped by life. Use me to point them in the direction of the exit. Allow me to share the love I have received from you so that they may find life worth living. Amen.

THE FACE OF GOD

Scripture: John 1:15-18

Text: *No man has ever seen God, but God the only Son, who is at the Father's side, has made him known (v. 18).*

A little girl was busily at work in her room drawing a picture. Her brother happened to come in and ask what she was doing.

"Drawing a picture of God," she replied.

"That's silly," said the brother, "no one knows what God looks like."

To this the little girl said, "They will when I get through with this picture!"

The word *God* is abstract by itself. Men in every generation have wondered what God is like. Wise men and philosophers have speculated about his character and activity. But John says the time of abstract speculation has come to an end. If we want to know what God is like, we look at Jesus. He has made God known.

This has direct implications for our living as disciples. It means that our task is to look carefully at the picture that has been drawn for us through Jesus. Unfortunately not everyone learns this. Some who come to Christ seem to think they must be continually trying to improve the picture, or even draw a new one that is more "relevant" for our time. Rather than studying the picture, they spend endless hours trying to make another one.

I hope it will be different for you—that your Christian life will be a time of studying the picture of God as it is painted for us in Jesus. And when you seek to introduce others to God, I hope you will hold up the picture of Jesus and invite them to look at him.

You and I have never seen God. But we have seen the best photograph of God ever made. We have seen Jesus.

Thank you, God, that you are not faceless. Thank you that in Jesus you have given me more than a concept. You have given me an example. Amen.

WHAT GOD NEEDS

Scripture: John 1:19-28

Text: *I am the voice of one calling in the desert (v. 23).*

I had finished preaching and was greeting people after the service. A man waited to approach me until nearly everyone else had left the church. But when he finally did, he said, "Preacher, I disagree with something you said tonight. You said that God needs people to help him do his work in the world. I don't believe that. God doesn't need you or me. If he wants to do something, he'll do it without any help from anyone."

I disagreed with the man then, and I would still disagree with him today. While it is obviously true that God is powerful enough to do anything he wants, it is also true (and clear from Scripture) that God has chosen us to accomplish his work in the world.

It is significant that John follows his description of the Word with the passage that describes John the Baptist's ministry. This tells me that God needs people who will be his voices.

I am quite certain that God could overwhelm us with a supernatural voice out of the sky. I have no doubt that he could bring all humanity to its knees with some cosmic demonstration. But when I look at the Bible, this is not how I see him working. He acts through the faithful witnessing of his people.

The book of John explains Christian discipleship. The world is like a desert. It is dry, parched, and dying for lack of people who will tell others about the Word. This passage combines with the first eighteen verses to tell us that the Word and witness belong together. What God needs is YOU!

Dear God, when I see your greatness may it not paralyze me

into inactivity. Rather, let it stir me to action. Let me never forget that even though you are powerful enough to work without me, you don't want to. I've known for a long time that I need you. It helps to know you need me, too. Amen.

FAITH AND SIGHT

Scripture: John 1:29-34

Text: *This is the one I meant when I said . . . (v. 30).*

Long before John the Baptist ever saw Jesus, he was telling others to get ready for him. John says he did not even know him, but he was sure he was coming. John trusted God enough to proclaim the message before Jesus ever arrived on the scene.

That's faith! Faith precedes sight and is sure even before it has a confirming experience. God honored that kind of faith with the encounter John was waiting for. One day there was Jesus—no doubt about it, and John exclaimed, "Behold the Lamb of God" (1:29, KJV). The one I knew was coming is here!

What about my faith? What about yours? Do we have faith that precedes sight, or do we just have faith in our sight? It makes all the difference in how far you are willing to launch out . . . how deep you are willing to go . . . what risks you are willing to take.

The writer of Hebrews said, "Now faith is being . . . certain of what we do not see" (11:1). Jesus said, "Blessed are those who have not seen and yet have believed" (20:29).

This kind of faith does not come overnight or easily. But we can be thankful the apostle John shows it to us early in his Gospel, so we may set our sights toward gaining it.

God, too often I have faith in my sight. Give me a faith that precedes sight. Give me faith to trust even before I see—and having seen, to testify. Amen.

COME AND SEE!

Scripture: John 1:35-39

Text: *Come, . . . and you will see (v. 39).*

How do you really find out about Jesus? How do you do more than just toy around with or play at being a Christian? This section of the Gospel gives us some answers.

For one thing, we must believe the proclamation. John the Baptist said, "Look, the Lamb of God" (1:29). John's disciples had to either accept or reject that. Someone today testifies about the truth and reality of Jesus. You hear it; then you must either believe it or not.

But even here we are just at the doorway to real experience. At the heart of encountering Christ are his words, "Come . . . and you will see." A passing glance is insufficient. Irregular contact will not breed lasting experience. Belief in someone else's witness will not bring about personal faith. There *must* be the willingness to become personally involved.

This is not surprising—it is this way in everything. Our whole educational system is built upon it. To really learn, you must become involved. Our employment system is founded on it. You may find out a lot *about* a certain field, but to really *know* it, you must work at it "on the job." The call to involvement is part and parcel of meaningful life at all levels. So too the life of faith.

But notice Jesus gives a promise—"Come and you *will* see." If you will get involved with him, you will know the truth. Before I married Jeannie, I believed I loved her. Since then, I have come and seen. Now I know I do. Before I walked with Christ, I believed he was the Son of God. I have come and seen. Now I know he is. Jeannie was always Jeannie. I just had to get to know her. Jesus has always been Jesus. I just had to know him. And I, you, and anyone else only get to know him by coming to him. When we come, we will see!

Jesus, forgive the times I have not been involved. Forgive my inconsistency in learning about so many things in life and yet trying to say I could not know you personally. Thank you for promising if I come I will see. I come. Amen.

GO AND TELL!

Scripture: John 1:40-52

Text: *The first thing Andrew did was to find his brother (v. 41).*

An experience with Jesus is founded on our willingness to come and see, and Jesus promises us we will see if we get personally involved. Following on the heels of those facts is the corollary truth: those who see will tell others.

This, too, is not foreign to other life experiences. Have you ever heard a record on the radio and just had to tell someone else? Have you ever been to the theater and been so moved by what you saw that you had to share it with someone? Have you been so captivated by a sunset that you could not keep it to yourself? All of us have known moving times that had to be shared. Not to share them is to crucify the experience.

So it is in coming to Christ and seeing. Andrew was one of John the Baptist's disciples. When invited by Jesus to "come and see," he was so caught up in the experience that John says, "The *first* thing Andrew did was to find his brother."

A little girl was so excited about having a new baby sister that she asked her mother if she could take her to school for "show and tell" time. The mother knew how much this meant to the girl and made arrangements for her to do it. When her turn came, she carefully wheeled the baby to the front, tilted the carriage, and exclaimed, "This is *my* baby sister!" May we be so in love with Jesus and excited about him that our first desire is to share him.

Lord, I am excited about you! And I really desire to have opportunities to tell others about you. Give me those opportunities. And when they come, let your Holy Spirit help me to let my inner desire and my outer witness be one. Amen.

DO ANYTHING!

Scripture: John 2:1-11

Text: *Do whatever he tells you (v. 5).*

What door must swing open before we can enter the world of the miraculous? Simply this: "Do whatever he tells you." There are no miracles unless we are willing to obey Jesus.

Willingness to do whatever he tells us opens us to our full potential of faith. Too often we try to draw boundary lines on what we will do for Christ and what we will allow him to do for us. We try to define how, when, and where he can be at work or how, when, and where we will be at work for him. To do whatever he tells us tears down all the barriers and makes every experience in life fair game for his presence.

Willingness to do whatever he tells us takes courage. It doesn't require much courage to ask God to rubber stamp your schemes. It doesn't take much courage to do only those things we know in advance are safe. But to do whatever he tells us means there may be some unusual things, some risky things. We may be misunderstood. We may not be liked by everyone. We may fail. Courage here allows Jesus to be at work in us and through us in ways he otherwise never could.

Do you have any empty jars in your life? If so, do whatever he tells you, and watch as they are filled to the brim with "the good wine"—experiences even better than before.

Lord, too often I have tried to get you to do whatever I told you. I have tried to call the shots. I must admit there have not been many miracles using that system. It looks like the only way is to do whatever you tell me. That may take some time. And it may take more courage than I have at this moment. But I believe you can and will help me. Amen.

MODERN-DAY TEMPLE CLEANSING

Scripture: John 2:12-25

Text: *Get these out of here! How dare you turn my Father's house into a market! (v. 16).*

"Popsicles for every child." "Credit cards honored in morning offering." "Spiritual trading stamps given for attendance." "One thousand balloons will be sent aloft from church parking lot." All these are publicity campaigns of local churches I have personally read about or seen. They make me wonder what Jesus would do if he happened to pass by.

The problem here is not the idea. We should always seek to make the gospel of Christ appealing. God help us that we don't demand long-faced narrow-mindedness as our ultimate test of faith. No, the problem here is not the idea. It is the fact that too often we place more emphasis on the gimmick than we do on the gospel. We spend more time trying to figure out ways to "get 'em here" than we do in making sure we have something for them when they come. We sacrifice the message on the altars of well-meaning novelty, compromise, and ease. We omit the weightier matters of commitment, cost, and sacrificial dedication.

Remember, the things that Jesus drove out of the temple started as good things. They were all services rendered to needy worshipers. The problem was that, in time, they evolved into opportunities to exploit people. Worship slipped into the background. This is what Jesus condemned.

He still does today. Be relevant? Yes. Be appealing? By all means! But never at the expense of the gospel. Never let the popsicles preempt the proclamation. Never let Master Charge cause us to forget the master's charge. We need to examine our priorities and motives. If we straighten things out, maybe

A FRESH START

Jesus won't have to pick up the whip again.

Lord, it's not easy to sweep those things out of my life that have glittered more than the gospel. Cliches instead of commitment. Tracts instead of testimony. The easy way instead of the narrow way. Sweat shirts instead of sweat. You know the rest, Jesus. And what goes for me goes for the church too, because I am the church. Help us to get down to business, before you have to give us the business. Amen.

THE HEART OF THE MATTER

Scripture: John 3:1-15

Text: *The wind blows wherever it pleases. You may hear its sound, but you cannot tell where it comes from or where it is going. So it is with everyone born of the Spirit (v. 8).*

It's so hard to get our eyes off the outward and spectacular Nicodemus had made a good observation about Jesus, but he had made it based on outward standards. When Jesus tried to take him to the heart of the matter—to things he could not see or measure—Nicodemus just couldn't grasp it.

We must be careful not to miss the transforming dimension of the gospel. In our day, we are tempted to judge effectiveness and greatness by outward standards. The standards of Christ, we must always remember, begin at the heart. Spiritual birth alone brings forth authentic spiritual life. Outward appearances and standards may look impressive; but unless they spring out of a heart touched by the Spirit, they are only self-generated.

The lesson in the cleansing of the Temple was that Jesus goes first to the inner motivations and inner life and uses what he sees there to judge the quality of outward performance. This truth, retold here in another way, should show us clearly what the first priority of the Christian is.

Every Christian is born twice, once physically—and again spiritually. We have a tangible physical birth, but the birth of the spirit is intangible. It is like the wind. We can't see it, but we can feel its effects and see what it does. Jesus is not minimizing outward signs; he is just letting us know that only the inner, spiritual birth is sufficient to bring outward fruit to maturity. This is still the heart of the matter.

A FRESH START

Heavenly Father, I have known what it is like to be active on the outside and empty in the heart. I can fake it for a while, but pretty soon there is nothing left to draw from. Let me start where you start—at the heart, and help me know if I can get right with you there, all the outer manifestations will find their place. Amen.

NO CONDEMNATION!

Scripture: John 3:16-21

Text: *God did not send his Son into the world to condemn the world, but to save the world through him (v. 17).*

A man said he did not like to look at pictures of Christ before he became a Christian. "When I did," he said, "Jesus always seemed to be saying, 'You shouldn't have done that.' " Even in the presence of a mere picture of Christ, the man felt guilty.

Many today feel uncomfortable in the presence of the master, but John says that Jesus did not come into the world to condemn anyone. He came to save everyone! It is not so much that Jesus' presence condemns us as it is that it is a *contrast* to the way we live. In his presence, we realize there is a better way, a different quality of life.

Just as sunlight appears more brilliant when we come out of a dark room, so our lives stand in greater contrast in the Lord's presence. John says some people choose to remain in the darkness. But if we will come to the light, we will find help and healing, for the light of Christ is that he "came to seek and to save what was lost" (Luke 19:10).

This is true liberation. It is freedom from bondage to ourselves and our past. To a world overturned with guilt, these words can be a message of great hope.

We have all heard John 3:16, but too often we stop reading there—just at the point where millions of people need to hear. For in verse 17, Christ comes offering salvation and saying, "You are not condemned!"

The man who once felt uncomfortable looking at pictures of Jesus went on to say that since becoming a Christian, pictures of Jesus seem to say, "Even when you are at your worst, *I love you!*" Instead of wanting to run from Christ, he now is drawn toward him.

A FRESH START

This is good news even for disciples, for there are times when we blow it. There are times when we need to come out of the darkness. For us, the offer is the same. The light of Christ is present to shine on any and all to fill our lives with peace and joy.

Today you will probably come in contact with people who don't like to look at pictures of Jesus. Offer them the message of John 3:17. Don't condemn them. Lead them to the place where they may know that Christ does not condemn them either. Lead them to the light—for salvation!

Heavenly Father, thank you for letting me know that you do not condemn me. This knowledge draws me toward you. Give me a sensitivity for those who may be crouching in the darkness, preferring that to your light. Let me lead them lovingly into the sunshine of healing love. Amen.

KEEP IT IN PERSPECTIVE!

Scripture: John 3:22-36

Text: *He must become greater; I must become less important (v. 30).*

One of the hardest things we ever have to do as Christians is to remember this verse. So easily and subtly we can lose this perspective on our faith.

In the beginning, it is not difficult to put our trust in Jesus. After all, we have never known anything like it before. But the days multiply, and as God's will becomes more and more the norm for our lives, we are tempted to forget to say thank you for the goodness of the Lord. And believe it or not, we sometimes begin to think we did it ourselves!

Something snaps when that happens. And unless we get hold of the situation and reverse it, it is the beginning of the end. The pages of history are strewn with cases of persons who started out right but ended up terribly wrong. One of the spiritual facts of life is that there are fewer people who make it to the end than there are who start the journey.

Somewhere in the course of events, ego gets too much in the way. Self-sufficiency raises its head again. Having stepped into the stream of the Spirit, we now find we have stepped back on the bank. The inevitable is happening—we are drying off!

What I write today is not meant to frighten—only to make you think. Spend this day letting these words of John the Baptist burn into your heart. They are the best safeguard against spiritual derailment.

God, you made me an individual. You gave me an ego. It's no sin to be me. It's no sin to think and choose. But, Lord, it is so easy to make the wrong choices and wind up trying to run things. Give me the sensitivity of spirit to keep my life in perspective. Help me to always allow you to be in control. Amen.

FROM DOUBT TO FAITH—1

Scripture: John 4:1-26

Text: *Jesus said to her, "Will you give me a drink?" (v. 7).*

We must spend a little time with this incident because there is so much here to help us grow in our faith. Let's consider this question: How do you overcome barriers to witnessing? It is so hard to penetrate past the defenses of people. In this passage we see some principles that can help us in the attempt. They are not sure-fire answers for every situation, but when prayerfully applied, they can be of great help to us.

First, there is *association*. Jesus associated with this woman. And when he did, he was in violation of Jewish law. No man was supposed to speak to a woman in public, much less a Jew to a Samaritan. That's why John tells us the disciples were surprised to find Jesus talking with the woman. Jesus began by daring to associate with her.

For some this is revolutionary. Too often we want to grab a person by the throat and say, "Brother, are you saved?" I heard one well-known preacher say, "We want to be hook-jammers instead of bait-danglers." To lead people from doubt to faith, however, we must learn to win the right to be heard. Taking time to associate with people—to show genuine interest—is the place to begin. Jesus did. Are we more impatient than he was? When we take time to associate with people and win their confidence, we begin to build the path from doubt to faith. It takes more time, but it treats people as people. And that's what witnessing is all about.

Ouch, God! I know what it feels like when someone tries to manipulate me. I can tell it when it's happening. It hurts. It makes me want to run. Save me from the sin of trying to do to others what I so despise having done to me. Instead, let me love people genuinely and be their friend. Then teach me to speak to them about my best Friend. Amen.

FROM DOUBT TO FAITH—2

Scripture: John 4:1-26

Text: *Sir, give me this water so that I won't get thirsty (v. 15).*

Jesus began his witness to the woman at the well not with a hard-sell approach, but with friendly association. But he didn't stop there, nor can we, lest we get the idea that mere presence is a full-fledged witness.

We see from the incident the second principle of *aroused interest*. After Jesus had established rapport, he looked for a point of need. Her need was to walk every day to and from town to draw water. Jesus picked up on this and began to talk about living water. She had never heard about this kind of water, and she was interested.

While water was not really her problem, it was a need to which Jesus could address himself. The discussion about living water formed the bridge between the immediate condition and the spiritual need. And this bridge aroused her interest so she wanted to hear more.

This kind of witness may not be easy. But for our witness to be effective, we must capture the interest of others. Pastor Bob Schuller of California has put it well when he says, "You have to find a need and fill it."

Part of the problem of ineffective witnessing may be that much of it is dull. It does not touch real needs. Jesus was not guilty of this. His witness was creative. It met needs.

After locating someone who does not know God, perhaps one of the first things we ought to pray is "God, what is there in this person's life I can touch with the gospel that will raise his or her interest?"

Father, a lot of what I try to pass off as witnessing is really boring when compared to Jesus' winsome testimony. Part of the problem may be that I have not taken time to really find how and where I can tap others' interests. Slow me down, Lord. Amen.

FROM DOUBT TO FAITH—3

Scripture: John 4:1-26

Text: *Go, call your husband (v. 15).*

By now I am sure you realize we are drinking from a deep well as we taste the living-water principles of witnessing. The water is cool, good, and satisfying. We must not stop drinking now. There is more.

The third element in our witnessing mosaic is the principle of *application.* Having associated with the woman and aroused her interest, Jesus moved to make the application he had intended to make all along. He spoke to the real need of the woman: her guilt over past experience, her present condition, and her resulting reputation. All these things were swirling around inside her. Jesus applied his living water to her need.

If our witnessing is to be effective, we too must make the application at some point; we must drive home the truth. Sometimes this is risky. But it must be done, or else we will never confront others with the necessity of a decision. In surgery, there must be cutting before there can be healing. In witnessing, there must be crystal-clear application before there can be conviction and decision.

Our problem is that we try to get there too fast. If you learn nothing else from these meditations, I hope you will see where this principle comes in the sequence. Not first, but third. The spiritual stranglehold we sometimes try to put on people must immediately be replaced by the calmer approach of winning a friend and arousing genuine interest. Then and only then can application be made and received. And the reception is what's all-important. It's easy to "jam the hook"—it takes holy patience and sensitivity to "catch the fish."

As we cultivate the friendship of others by association, and as we draw out desire and interest in them, let us be asking the

Spirit for that moment when, by his grace, we can get the point across.

God, premature applications only alienate people. Failure to make applications leaves people dangling. Enable me to make the application that needs to be made in a way that will strike a note of acceptance. Amen.

FROM DOUBT TO FAITH—4

Scripture: John 4:1-26

Text: *Believe me, woman, a time is coming when you will worship the Father neither on this mountain nor in Jerusalem (v. 21).*

When Jesus made the application plain, the woman's tendency was to change the subject. She did not want to see herself as she really was, so she shifted the issue over to true and false worship.

It is a psychological fact that the hardest truth to accept is truth about ourselves. As we witness, we will find that the general pattern is for people to start changing the subject when we get close to home. On one occasion when I was sharing the gospel and had made the application, the person responded with this question: "But what about the people in Africa who have never heard?" Good question. But not the issue. The woman at the well had a good observation about worship, but if Jesus had followed her, the witness would have stalled right there. Instead, he stuck to the issue and amplified it.

The path from doubt to faith is not without its detours. For some strange reason, we go great distances to keep from dealing with our deepest needs. A witness can spend a lifetime dealing with side issues, all of which seem good. Or he can stick to the main issue at hand and lead men and women to the place where they must consider Jesus personally. Remember, the application was the hardest part for most people. If you have gone that far, don't let secondary issues defeat you.

Lord, it's easy to get sidetracked, especially when people wonder about things I have wondered about too. Help me to remember that I am not there to speculate but to proclaim. Amen.

FROM DOUBT TO FAITH—5

Scripture: John 4:1-26

Text: *I who speak to you am he (v. 26).*

One overarching truth is evident in this episode—throughout the entire witness presentation, Jesus *declared good news*. He was positive. From the moment he saw the woman, he saw her not for what she was but for what she could become. In that spirit he related himself to her. He based the content of his witness on the possibility of change. And she changed.

Jesus was demonstrating an important principle: people respond as much to *how* we say something as to *what* we say. If we are open, our listener will tend to be open. If we are confident, we breed confidence. If we believe in them, they believe in themselves. The reverse is also true.

Too often our witnessing has been like the person who heard of his friend's illness, went to the home and, in an attempt to be consoling, said, "I've known three people with this disease, and one of them lived." It may have been true, but it was not very good news.

Somewhere along the line too many Christians have become experts in problem analysis. We can spend thirty minutes on what's wrong, but have trouble coming up with two minutes of how it can be made right. We can point out the possibility of hell, but can't describe the joys of heaven.

Remember Jesus. He declared good news! In the witness section of his *Evangelism Explosion* plan, Dr. James Kennedy has the witness turn to the prospect and say, "Mr. Jones, a few minutes ago I said I might have good news to share with you; now I know I do!" Positive. Good news. People have already heard all the bad news they want to hear. They know all the bad things about themselves they want to know (even if they won't admit it). But people are desperate for good news—and that's what the gospel is.

Heavenly Father, give me good news eyes, good news ears, a good news mind, and a good news mouth. Amen.

YOU NEED TO KNOW THIS MAN!

Scripture: John 4:27-38

Text: *Come, see a man who told me everything I ever did (v. 29).*

Wouldn't it blow your mind if today you had a conversation with someone who told you things about yourself only you knew? It blew the mind of the woman at the well too. She left her water pots and ran into town to tell others about Jesus.

There are several insights here for us. First, the fact that Christ knows all about us is a liberating truth. We have already seen that although it hurt to know the truth, when it was all out in the open, this woman was set free to live in a way she had never been able to live before. We feel relief and joy when we know Jesus knows all about us.

Second, the woman's inhibitions were dropped. Previously she had been afraid to be seen in public. She was even drawing water at an unusual hour to avoid others. She never would have dreamed of going up to people and speaking this way. But when she knew that Jesus knew all about her and loved her, she could love and accept herself. She did not have to cower anymore. She was free.

Third, she was genuine. Ordinarily people would have laughed in her face—or spit in it. But now they listened. And what's even more incredible, they believed. She was different. The change worked in her life because of her encounter with Christ was no cosmetic, superficial job. She was a new creation! People could tell it, and they wanted to meet someone who could transform a woman like that.

There is no regret when we realize Jesus knows all about us. Instead, there are rejoicing and liberation. There is the desire to tell others, "You need to know this man."

God, I guess I've always intellectually believed you know all about me. But now I feel that truth sinking in. And, you know, it doesn't scare me. It makes me feel better. And it makes me feel like there are others who would feel better too if they only knew it. Lead me to someone to whom I can say, "Come, see this man who told me everything I ever did." Amen.

WHERE IT ALL WINDS UP

Scripture: John 4:39-42

Text: *We no longer believe just because of what you said; now we have heard for ourselves, and we know that this man really is the Savior of the world (v. 42).*

No more beautiful words can be heard by a witness than these. This is where we hope and pray it will all wind up. This is the place where new spiritual life has been reproduced. It is the place where people begin to believe for themselves.

At best, a witness is used of God to open the door of faith in another. Others may believe everything we say. They may decide for Jesus on the basis of it. But at that point they are still believing primarily on our experience. They need one of their own.

Notice that John tells us there were many who believed because of the woman's testimony. That in itself is great. The townspeople in this story went a step further. They went out to see Jesus and hear him for themselves. He stayed with them for two days, and that encounter brought even deeper faith and commitment.

It will do the same for your friends and neighbors too. They may make genuine decisions because you witnessed to them. They may go with you as you continue to disciple them and follow them up. But the greatest step will be the day when one of them comes in all excited and says without your having said anything, "I've just got to tell you what Jesus has been doing for me!" When that happens, you can whisper a silent "Thank you, Lord," for you will know that all the days, effort, and prayers have led your dear friend to the feet of Jesus.

Lord, I am thankful for those who have come to faith because of my testimony. I don't ever want to stop giving it when I have the chance. But, Lord, it's music to my ears to hear someone tell me of a personal encounter. That's what it's all about, Lord. Help me to stick with people until it happens. Amen.

THE HEALING CHRIST

Scripture: John 4:43-54

Text: *You may go. Your son will live (v. 50).*

The healing Christ. This is our first glimpse of him in this Gospel. Perhaps you have never seen him before. Today see the Christ who is able to heal with the spoken word. No elaborate or mystical activity here—just power. Power to say the word that makes a body whole.

But there is something else here—faith. The faith of the royal official. He wanted Jesus to go with him to his home. When Jesus indicated that he was not going to go, it would have been natural for the man to be discouraged. When Jesus told the man his son would live, it would have been natural to react sarcastically. The official could have left feeling worse than ever, and believing Jesus did not really care.

But not this man! He left believing. He took Jesus at his word. His first step toward home without Jesus was proof he believed. And his faith was rewarded with a healed son. But the story does not stop there. That kind of healing makes waves. The entire household of this official came to believe because of it.

Behold the healing Christ! Realize that he is not bound by distance. He is not limited to a set way of doing anything. The only limiting obstacle he faces is our faith. We can win or lose at that point. But when the power of the healing Christ is combined with our faith, mountains can be moved.

Heavenly Father, I know there are many mysteries about healing. I know there is much I do not understand. But help me to get a vision of the powerful, healing Jesus. I have some mountains that need moving too. Amen.

IT DOESN'T COME EASY

Scripture: John 5:1-15

Text: *One who was there had been an invalid for thirty-eight years (v. 5).*

It is significant that this story follows the account of the healing of the official's son—an instantaneous healing that took place just by the spoken word. But this event is quite different, and the point is well made that healing and deliverance do not always come easily. We make a mistake to think so.

This man had lain by the pool for thirty-eight years. He was probably a teenager or young adult when he was left there, so when Jesus came he was probably middle-aged at least. Most people would have given up before then.

It may be that he had given up too, for the first question Jesus asked was, "Do you want to get well?" That seems like a strange question, but it was *crucial*. After thirty-eight years, faith can be as dry as the desert sand. After thirty-eight years, we can be so used to people waiting on us that we have come to expect it. After thirty-eight years of inactivity, it can be frightening to know we must suddenly make our own way in the world. So the question is vital. It may be that all the talk of wanting to be healed was just a cover-up, or perhaps, he really wanted to be well again. Jesus wanted to find out which.

Evidently the man did want healing, and Jesus worked the miracle that transformed the man's life. A door swung open that day, and he was alive in a way he had never been before.

As we minister to people, we must remember that not everyone wants deliverance. Some just want sympathy. As we minister, we must remember that all healing is not instantaneous. We create barriers to faith by giving the false impression that it is. But if any of us sincerely want to be delivered, there is one who is able. Again we see that when his ability is unleashed by our willingness, miracles happen!

Lord, is there anyone I will meet today who needs deliverance? If so, show me. And as I seek to help others find wholeness of life, save me from making it look cheap, quick, and easy. Lord, we live in an instant society. Sometimes it is hard to wait for anything. Help me to help others see that it is depth of faith, not length of time, that really matters. Amen.

I AND MY FATHER

Scripture: John 5:16-30

Text: *He was even calling God his own Father, making himself equal with God (v. 18).*

This is one of those passages that is equally beautiful and difficult. Beautiful because it so clearly states the relationship of Jesus to the Father. Difficult because it is so hard for people to understand and accept. Just about everyone can accept Jesus as a great man, wise teacher, and profound philosopher. But not everyone buys the Christian teaching that God was in him—that he was God in the flesh. Yet, that is what he dared to teach. It is what Christianity dares to proclaim. You may have to spend a lot of time here pondering these truths for yourself, but today let us see the things that Jesus teaches about his relationship to the Father:

- equality
- partnership
- life-giving resurrection
- mutual honor
- authority and judgment

His claims really got to the Jews and offended them so much that they sought ways to kill Jesus. This kind of truth will still be offensive to some. Because when you admit that Jesus is the Son of God, you are immediately accountable to him. People would rather reduce him to their size and ignore him. Many do. But the glorious truth is that when we accept him for who he says he is and relate ourselves to him, we are changed!

Father, thank you for coming to us in the person of Jesus. Because of him I know you—I encounter you. Amen.

STUBBORN REFUSAL

Scripture: John 5:31-47

Text: *Yet you refuse to come to me to have life (v. 40).*

Some people refuse to believe, even in the face of evidence. Perhaps you can recall man's first steps on the moon and the pictures of that event. I remember reading an article several days later that said there were people who refused to accept the moon landing as fact. They were saying it was all staged in a television studio!

Jesus faced the same kind of mentality. He had performed signs and wonders. He had been announced by John the Baptist. The Scriptures had predicted his coming as Messiah. Yet there were those who preferred to cling to their own narrow-mindedness. This spirit is not dead even after two thousand years. Perhaps you have met people who firmly believe their judgment concerning Christ and the Christian faith is more valid than your witness, two thousand years of church history, and the testimony of Scripture.

What does Jesus say? He says the very standards that have been used to deny him will one day rise up to accuse those who have denied him. And that is the supreme irony of life! The very things we cling to in order to avoid dealing with Christ will one day be the jury that declares us guilty. Jesus will not have to condemn us—we will have condemned ourselves. Our own stubborn wills and self-righteousness will make up the panel. Sobering thought, isn't it? Maybe one more consideration of Jesus would not hurt.

Heavenly Father, I wonder how many times I have set up my standards and said they were superior to yours. Forgive the times I have done so. Open my eyes that I may see. Amen.

YOU CAN'T MAKE HIM!

Scripture: John 6:1-15

Text: *They intended to come and make him king by force (v. 15).*

We are in familiar territory in this section of the Gospel. Nearly everyone knows about the feeding of the five thousand. The usual focus of the passage is on the miracle, and the point is sometimes made that Jesus can do a lot with a little—that he can do a lot with the little bit that you and I surrender to him.

While I am sure that is true, let's look at something else—the end of the story, where the people try to force Jesus to be their king. What did he do? John says, "Jesus . . . withdrew again into the hills by himself" (v. 15).

Did Jesus withdraw because he was not a king? Of course not. He was, and is, King of Kings. He withdrew because of what they expected him to be as their king. They could not make him a king when *king* meant something different from what Jesus meant.

There is a tremendous lesson here—we cannot force the hand of God. Have you ever been so sure God should do something that you almost said, "Come on, God, be God!" And just like Jesus' experience, it is not that God is not God—it is that he is not the kind of god we have in mind. We cannot make him be what he is not, even if you call him "God." We cannot dictate to God what he must do, or when. We cannot impose our will on him and ask him to rubber stamp it.

Not long ago I heard a song that tried to do this. I do not remember all the words of the song, but one line was repeated over and over—"It must be the will of the Lord, because it seems so right to me." Isn't that what the people were thinking as they tried to make Jesus king?

It is not a matter of making him our king, but rather of

allowing him to be the king that he already is. We don't need to define his lordship. We just need to let him be Lord. When we do that, he will not withdraw from us. He will come to us in power, and we will declare, "This man is king indeed!"

Lord, forgive the times I have tried to "lord it over you" by trying to make you what I wanted you to be. Then I wonder why you seem to disappear. Now I know. I offer my life to you today and ask you to be Lord of it—with no strings attached. Amen.

FEAR NOT!

Scripture: John 6:16-24

Text: *It is I; don't be afraid (v. 20).*

Do you have any fears? Is there something in your life today that terrifies you or renders you useless as far as production in the Kingdom of God is concerned?

I can still remember what it was in my life. When I was in high school, I was terrified at having to stand before a class and give a book report, recite a poem, or make a speech. I remember one time I had cut my chin in an accident, and I told the teacher that the doctor had told me not to talk much until it healed. It was a bald-faced lie, but it got me out of a book report!

This fear came to a peak when, in my sophomore year, I was converted and shortly after that received a definite call to the ordained ministry. I was gripped with a fear I cannot describe, because I knew one of the things preachers had to do was speak—often and to many different kinds of audiences. My fear said, "No way! Not you! Never!" But the call was still there and it would not go away.

Into that confusing mixture of call and chaos Jesus came, walking on the rough seas of my life. And while I did not hear an audible voice, he spoke the words of our text today, "It is I; don't be afraid." He was saying to me, "Steve, I am in this, and because that is so you don't have anything to fear." I cannot say that upon hearing that word my fear vanished. For some time there was a struggle between my faith and my fear. But as the call remained, and as the assurance lingered, my fear began to dissolve.

In sharing with many others over the years, I have discovered that my fears, my feelings about them, and the ways I try to deal with them are fairly common among God's people.

A FRESH START

Many Christians are asked to do things that terrify them. They refuse. And the result is a guilt-producing, anxiety-fostering attitude that only feeds the fear more and builds up a higher wall of frustration. Somehow this cycle must be broken, and I believe it can be. How?

First, do you have a fear? Name it. Get it out in the open, into the light. Just like creepy insects, most fears run for the cover of darkness when exposed. Share it with someone else, and ask them to pray with you about it.

Second, is that fear preventing you from performing some service for God? Perhaps it is a fear of rejection, so you do not witness or teach a Sunday school class. Maybe your fear is like mine was, and so you never get in a position in which you have to pray or talk in a group. Maybe it's a fear of failure, so rather than fail, you never attempt anything for God. Maybe it's one of a thousand other things. But do those fears cause you to hide your talents under a bucket? If so, confess that before God.

Third, chances are you may be called by God at the point of your specific fear to allow him to help you overcome it. Just as with the disciples, Christ is willing to walk with you on your rough seas and say, "It is I; don't be afraid." Are you willing to hang on to your calling more than your fear? You should be for our Lord's sake.

Fourth, are you willing to experiment a little? You will never overcome your fear, even with Christ's help, until you are willing to make some kind of break with your past. You don't have to conquer the world tomorrow. But you do have to move out a little. In my particular fear of speaking, I first ventured out with a brief program at the youth group, then a Sunday school lesson, and then my first sermon in friendly surroundings. It is in our willingness to venture out that we receive confirmation that God is really with us. It won't be easy, and it may take time, but this experimentation is where the beachhead of victory is established.

Many people have fears that run them aground and scuttle their discipleship. It does not have to be so. Christ is with you today—fear not!

Lord, come upon the tossing waves of my fear. Calm my troubled soul. Help me to overcome my fears so that I may more effectively, joyfully, and faithfully serve you. Amen.

BELIEVE!

Scripture: John 6: 25-29

Text: *The work of God is this: to believe in the one whom he has sent* (v. 29).

It's been around a long time—the feeling that there is some immeasurable amount of activity that must be performed before we can please God or be effective for him. It was there with Jesus two thousand years ago, and I am still amazed today at how many people try to make Christianity and going to heaven contingent on "doing the best you can."

The crowd asked Jesus, "What must we do to do the work of God?" (v. 28). What must we *do?* The answer Jesus gave is the text for our thought today. And his answer was that the real work is believing. Let's think about what that means.

For one thing, being precedes doing. A Christian is first a person who *is* something, not one who *does* something. Character is the root of conduct. More than once I have heard people testify, "I tried to live the Christian life before I became a Christian."

But there's something else. Belief is more than intellectual assent. Jesus says it is a work, a participation in what God is doing. And this belief has a clear object—the one God sent— Jesus. To do God's work is to be involved in the work of Christ through trusting in him as our only hope and the world's only salvation.

Belief a work? To a culture that ingrains in us the idea that the only way to make it is to achieve with blood, sweat, and tears, that sounds ridiculous. Belief a work? To churches that measure discipleship primarily by attendance and holding offices, it just doesn't seem to get the job done. To some who don't believe you are a Christian until you are involved in struggle for social change, these words seem absurd.

Don't get me wrong; don't isolate this meditation and try to make it the be-all and end-all. Certainly there is a place for actually working for the Lord. Sure we need to be present in the Lord's house and involved in the organization that helps accomplish his will. You bet the church had better speak out against injustice and oppression. But Jesus reminds us that all these "works," good as they are, can never substitute for personal belief in him.

Even as I write this I realize I have so much to do. But as you and I leave this time together to do our work, let's remember that our primary work—the work of God—is to believe in Jesus and to let that belief saturate all else that we do.

Father, set me to work today—believing. And let that faith be the foundation and the guidance for all I attempt to do. Amen.

FRESH BREAD

Scripture: John 6:30-59

Text: *I am the bread of life (v. 35).*

Not far from the college I attended there was a commercial bakery. When the wind was right, the aroma of freshly baked bread would float over the campus. Like the tune of a piper, that smell would lure our appetites. I am sure that there were many evenings when that odor alone accounted for increased sales at the nearby drive-ins. Even today I still enjoy the smell of bread baking or opening a new loaf, smelling and feeling it—then eating it!

Jesus used this image when he described himself as the bread of life. Many who heard him could not accept this phrase and were offended. As we read this passage we can sense the increasing hostility. But for a growing faith and fruitful discipleship, no real progress can be made without nourishment from God through Jesus Christ, the bread of life.

First, bread is a relational object. Bread does no good until you eat it. To just smell and gaze at a loaf of bread is not very satisfying. You can starve to death with loaves of bread piled around you. To be nourished by bread you must take it into yourself and let it do its work.

The same is true for the bread of life. We must allow Jesus to enter our lives and do his work. Just as there is a relationship between the bread and the eater, so a relationship must be established between the disciple and Jesus.

Second, bread must be eaten regularly. I would have been dead long ago if I had tried to live on the memory of that bakery. We will dry up and wither if we try to live on yesterday's feasting or last year's experience. Bread must be taken daily, and the vital disciple will return daily to the feet of Jesus and be fed by him.

Third, the bread satisfies. Our baby book at home says that toddlers love bread and butter sandwiches better than anything else. Our three-year-old has confirmed that truth. He can say, "Mommy, I'm starving." But satisfaction is just a bread slice away! Jesus dares to claim that, "He who comes to me will never go hungry." Life's spiritual satisfaction for now and eternity is found in Jesus.

And so he said, "Unless you eat the flesh of the Son of Man and drink his blood, you have no life in you" (v. 53). Most see some reference to the sacrament here and I'm sure that's true. But certainly Jesus also meant that real life for the Christian is found as we take into ourselves the life of the Son of man as surely as we take into ourselves the bread from our table.

Heavenly Father, I'm hungry. Thank you for the food you will give me today to satisfy that hunger and nourish my body. Lord, my spirit is hungry too. Thank you that you took that hunger into account and sent Jesus to be the bread for my life. As I go through this day, help me to feast on that bread even as I feast on the food from my table. Amen.

HANG IN THERE

Scripture: John 6:60-70

Text: *This is a hard teaching. Who can accept it? (v. 60).*

In the locker room of our high school fieldhouse this slogan hung: "When the going gets tough, the tough get going." The obvious implication was that when the heat really gets on, only the truly committed hang in there; others drop out. Every time we saw that phrase we had to make up our minds which we were.

By reading John's Gospel, we are beginning to catch something of what Jesus is holding out as authentic Christianity. We are beginning to see how all-encompassing Christian discipleship really is. When Jesus finished sharing some of these things, "many of his disciples turned back and no longer followed him" (v. 66).

What about you? What about me? What are we going to do? Jesus asks us, "Do you also want to leave?" Have you made up your mind? Have I?

While there are many possible answers we could give, only one will keep our Christian experience going. It is the answer Peter gave. "Lord, to whom shall we go? You have the words of eternal life. We believe and know that you are the Holy One of God" (vv. 68, 69).

And in my most honest moments I have to agree. I've come far enough in my Christian faith to know that turning back is not really a serious option. I would be miserable if I forsook the life I have come to know. I would be foolish to leave the one who changed and changes me.

Maybe you're like me. Maybe you get tired of trying to live it. Maybe you get frustrated by your imperfect performance. Maybe you get overwhelmed by the magnitude of what you're involved in. Hang in there! When the going gets tough, the tough get going. You've got the best coach, the most workable game plan, and a whole world full of teammates who are also struggling to improve their game. Go out onto the field today knowing he's with you. He will be until the end of the world.

Lord, I really need help today. I need it because there are times when your sayings get pretty hard. Hard to accept. Harder to live out. It's tough, Lord. But you know that—because you lived here and had it a lot worse than I do. I can't make any glowing promises about tomorrow, next week, or next year. But I am willing to hang in there today. Amen.

STIFLED

Scripture: John 7:1-13

Text: *No one would say anything publicly about him for fear of the Jews (v. 13).*

No one would say anything publicly about him for *fear*. For fear of what? You fill in the blanks. For fear of rejection. For fear of ridicule. For fear of reputation. For fear of position. You name it.

It is not uncommon to find people who hold to the "keep Jesus to yourself" philosophy. They give many reasons for their position. "What right do we have to go to others about Christ? People know where the church is if they want it." "After all, one belief is as good as another so long as you're sincere." "Religion is a personal matter."

That last statement reminds me of the fellow I heard about who said that in his home as a child, religion was a personal matter—so personal he doubted if anyone had any.

Our reasons for not sharing our faith are often not because of our feelings about others but because of the fear we have in ourselves. We are stifled, and to cover up we devise noble rationalizations about the rights of others, etc.

But wait! A witness for Jesus Christ presented in love through word and deed is not the offensive part. The offensive part is professing to believe in Jesus Christ and yet keeping him to ourselves. The offensive part is claiming to know Christ and yet living as if we don't. That's what really turns people off. That's what makes the world criticize us for talking a better game than we play. It's the so-called Christians who compromise their convictions in daily living who turn people away.

When I was in India I rode with church leaders on the train from village to village. As we rode, one leader shared a tragic story with us. He told how some of the pastors and church officers were mishandling funds by selling blankets and clothing that mission agencies sent for children. I asked the man, "What do the Hindus and Muslims in your city think about that?"

"They no longer take our religion seriously," he replied. "They are more ethical and honest with their many gods than the Christians are with their one God; they see no need to change." My heart fell.

"No one would say anything publicly about him for fear. . . ." Surely there is no greater need in our society than for Christians who will dare to live their faith before others. Yes, risk is involved, but Christianity cannot survive unless we do.

Dear God, there are many reasons why I fear to publicly live my faith. I am prone to take the way of least resistance. Help me to see that while I do this the world is dying for lack of a positive witness for Christ. As I live this day, may I dare to let the principles of the Christian life guide my actions. Amen.

THE ONLY VALID SOURCE

Scripture: John 7:14-24

Text: *My teaching is not my own. It comes from him who sent me (v. 16).*

What is the source of our teaching? In a day when so many "brands" of Christianity are going around, this is one of the most important questions we can ask ourselves. This verse implies two possibilities. Our teaching can come from God, or it can come from ourselves. Jesus says the person who speaks on his own does so to glorify himself. Only the person who has God as his source glorifies him.

This problem existed even in Jeremiah's day—about 600 B.C. He said of false prophets, "They speak visions from their own minds, not from the mouth of the Lord" (Jer. 23:16). They had the wrong source, and as a result, an entire nation was led down the road to captivity.

I have a friend who came out of seminary with practically no faith and certainly no personal experience of Jesus. For several years he tried to preach, but his messages were sterile; they came out of his best mental efforts to do a job, not out of inspiration through a relationship with God. He became increasingly frustrated with the condition of his life and the gap between what he had to tell people on Sunday and what he believed and lived the rest of the week. Late one Saturday night, he turned to his wife and said, "Honey, I've got to go down to the church for a while." For the next several hours he agonized before God. The victory came! He made the switch to a new source, a source he had never before had in his life or ministry. And today he is alive to God and being used by him. Discovering the source made all the difference.

Two men were to recite Psalm 23 at a public meeting. One was a skilled orator; the other was a much-loved man in the community. The orator rose and with golden-tongued eloquence gave a recitation of the psalm that brought the crowd to its feet with deafening applause. Then the second man rose to say the psalm. He lacked the professional skill of the first man, but when he finished the crowd was moved to silence—the kind of silence you feel when something significant has happened. The orator broke the silence with these words. "When I stood to recite Psalm 23 you applauded. When this man shared it, you were silent. What is the difference? I'll tell you. I know the psalm, but he knows the Shepherd."

That's still the difference today. Our source makes all the difference. Are we just parroting truth to be heard of men, or are we saturated by truth to be used of God?

Lord, I know the only way I can be growing in my faith is to allow you to be my source. Help me not only to know about you, but to know you in a personal, daily relationship. Enable me by your Spirit not just to parrot truth, but to be of the truth. Amen.

COOL, CLEAR WATER

Scripture: John 7: 25-44

Text: *If a man is thirsty, let him come to me and drink (v. 37).*

As I write this, an eight-year-old boy has just been found after being lost in rugged ranch country. He wandered for forty-two hours before he was located. Some of the time the temperature dropped below freezing. When he was found he was tired, hungry, and thirsty. Jesus says spiritual wandering makes us thirsty. He invites such wanderers to come to him and drink.

One evening in a revival a young man came and knelt at the altar. As is my custom, I asked, "Why did you come?"

For a moment he didn't say anything. Then he said, "I've been wandering away from God and I'm so tired of it. I want to come back." And he did. That night his grandmother, mother, and wife were also gloriously touched by the Spirit of God! Jesus says if you're tired and thirsty from wandering, come to him and drink.

But he goes farther. He says that coming to him can make a well of living water spring up in us. I saw an artesian spring by the edge of a highway at an attractive roadside park. Signs publicized it well in advance, and many travelers stopped to drink the cool, clear water.

Jesus says it can be that way with us. We can have an artesian spring always flowing in our lives. From it we can be nourished, and others will find nourishment also. That well is the spring of the Spirit.

Jesus does not just offer a drink. He offers a well, and in this lies the secret of discipleship. A single drink will soon be exhausted and forgotten. But a well can be drawn from daily. There is an abundance for ourselves and others. Today is a good day to ask him to begin digging that well in our lives.

Lord, let me hear a beautiful sound—the sound of drilling. Then let me hear the beautiful sound of bubbling—the bubbling, flowing sound your Spirit makes when he overflows a life. Lord, I am thirsty. I need a drink. But even more I need a well. Amen.

A UNIQUE SPEAKER

Scripture: John 7:45-53

Text: *No one ever spoke the way this man does (v. 46).*

"The pen is mightier than the sword." The word is stronger than the weapon. The words of Jesus subdued the temple guards sent to arrest him. They came back with one message, "No one ever spoke the way he does."

But it's not just any word that has this effect. Our world is saturated with words—legislation, negotiation, resolutions, laws, decrees, pronouncements—an avalanche of words! But wars continue, violence goes on, people are still oppressed. No, not just any words will do. The world chants the childhood rhyme, "Sticks and stones may break my bones, but words will never hurt me."

But there *is* a word . . . no, Word. The Word of God. It still has the power to bring rulers to their knees, to calm troubled lives, to put people back together.

Charles Colson, who was President Nixon's dirty-tricks man, was speaking before a group of businessmen. He said that during those years of preparing many words and doing many things, he could not remember one constructive thing he had done or one single life he had affected positively. But then he was won to Christ, and now he says his testimony has brought piles of letters from people who have been influenced by what he says and how he lives.

Every one of us has the same choice Colson had. We can spend a lifetime uttering words, and when we're gone few will remember. Or we can take the Word of God upon our lips and spend a lifetime sharing it. If we choose to do this, untold lives will be touched and eternally affected.

Lord, place your Word on my tongue. Amen.

GO AND SIN NO MORE

Scripture: John 8:1-11

Text: *Teacher, this woman was caught in the act of adultery (v. 4).*

Caught in the act. Even in a society that excuses so much sin, these are words of indictment. To many people, sin is getting caught. These words leave no doubt about the guilt to anyone.

How many times have we been caught in the act? Oh, we've all had our share of experiences of being caught with our hand in the cookie jar. We have all had our personal repenting to do for the sins we committed that others knew about. Even our nation has had to go through a painful process as a result of being caught. But what about those times when we weren't caught by people, when only God knew? That makes the list considerably longer. On the side of the ledger marked "Blown It" are more than enough entries for each of us.

But there is more in this story than guilt and condemnation. If there hadn't been, we would have heard the screams of the woman as she died under the rock pile, according to Law. We can be thankful there is another power at work, the power of forgiveness and transformation. And that power is greater than the power of sin, judgment, and law.

Note that the sin was not excused. It never is. The woman had sinned; she was guilty. We have sinned; we are guilty. Death is the deserved outcome (Rom. 6:23) if you go only by Law. But mercy looks to the future and capitalizes on the willingness to change.

Yet even forgiveness is not unconditional or automatic. The stipulation is that we "go, and sin no more" (John 8:11, KJV). We get our hand out of the cookie jar and don't put it back in again. There must be a determination to change before there can be a declaration of forgiveness. And that's not an easy proposition. But it is the only way not to get caught again.

A FRESH START

Lord, I have sinned. I am a sinner. You've got me red-handed. I deserve judgment if we play it strictly by the book. But thank you, Lord, that there is an alternative, the alternative of mercy. I opt for that alternative. In return, I leave the sin behind to live in the glorious light of your forgiveness. Amen.

LET THERE BE LIGHT

Scripture: John 8:12-30

Text: *I am the light of the world (v. 12).*

Mammoth Cave in southwestern Kentucky is the largest cave of its type in the world. During our seminary days, my wife, Jeannie, and I took the five-mile tour that included a stop in a large room in the cave. When we tourists were all together, the ranger said, "Please turn out all your flashlights and extinguish all cigarettes. In a moment I am going to turn out the lights. For some of you this will be your first experience in total darkness." I have been in dark places before, but never anything like that. You literally could not see your hand in front of your face. It was a darkness you could feel. We were all relieved when the lights came on again.

What a difference light can make. Much needless stumbling is prevented by it. Fear of many unknowns is dispelled. We are able to see and have some bearings on life.

It can be dark in our spirits too. We can stumble around in our spiritual life. Many people are doing that today as they grope for spiritual reality and answers in weird and wrong places. We need light—light that can lift the blanket of darkness. And the good news of the gospel of Jesus Christ is that light has come! Jesus is the light; we need not stumble in darkness anymore!

This truth was graphically illustrated for me when I was preaching to youth in a camp meeting in Michigan. During the evening session, it began to pour down rain. Jeannie motioned to me that she was going to our room. I stayed behind a while longer. By the time I left, the rain had slackened some, but the ground was soaked, and puddles were everywhere. Jeannie had taken the flashlight, and there were no lights between the tabernacle and our room. The next minutes were a frustrating series of stumbles and sinking into waterholes over my shoes. When I got there I was soaked. How many times I wished for that flashlight! What a difference it would have made!

Whether we are Christian or not, life has its mudholes and unexpected low places. The difference is in whether we have light. Today there is light for our walk—Jesus.

Father, I have so much trouble walking in the darkness. You know that. Thank you that in Jesus you have given me light. You have told me that as he lives in me, I am the light of the world too. Today let me walk by his light and reflect it so that others may stop their stumbling. Amen.

FIND FREEDOM

Scripture: John 8: 31-41

Text: *You will know the truth, and the truth will set you free (v. 32).*

A hit song a few years ago said, "I want to be free." A national best seller was about a seagull who learned the joy and freedom of soaring. Martin Luther King, Jr., had a dream when one day all mankind could exclaim, "Free at last! Free at last! Thank God, we're free at last!"

Whenever you talk about, sing about, or write about freedom, you have tapped the human spirit. We want to be free. This intense human desire has forced oppressive governments to put up walls that confine. Those who have abused freedom have had to be restricted behind bars. Desire for freedom has led to and generated mankind's most notable achievements and heartbreaking failures.

An interesting sequence of thought runs through the Gospel of John. First, we need to know the truth. Second, truth gives us real freedom. So far this sounds like any notable philosophy of life, but what makes this teaching distinctively Christian is the third thought: Jesus declares, "I am . . . the truth" (14: 6).

That's different! No philosophy can stand up to it. Truth is no longer abstract, no longer conceptual, but immediate. It has been fleshed out and made real through a person. The distinctive thing about Christianity as opposed to other religions and philosophies is that the Word became flesh; word did not remain word. So if truth can find expression through a real person, then truth can find expression through me as that person resides in my life. That is freedom!

There is a little Jonathan Livingston Seagull in all of us. Jesus speaks to that part of our lives and says that if we are to be free, really free, we must relate to him. Break free today and let Jesus break in.

A FRESH START

"Into my heart, into my heart. Come into my heart, Lord Jesus. Come in today. Come in to stay. Come into my heart, Lord Jesus." Then I shall be free at last! Amen.

FINAL PROOF

Scripture: John 8:42-47

Text: *If God were your Father, you would love me, for I came from God (v. 42).*

America is in danger of redefining Christianity into a cultural folk religion, not unlike ancient Greece did before its decline. A survey reveals that over 90 percent of the people polled believe in God (as they understand the word), but less than 35 percent say they allow that God to have any guiding hand in their lives. Being a good, moral, law-abiding, tax-paying citizen is a definition of religion (even Christianity?) for some. In some circles, being a patriotic American equals being a good Christian. A tragic blurring has occurred in some people's vision.

The same was true for the Jews of Jesus' day. Some said, "The Jews are God's chosen people, so all you have to do to be God's child is to be a good Jew."

Jesus replied, "Not so!" He went to great lengths to get one point across: there is an indispensible link between faith in God and belief in Christ. He stripped away the cultural barnacles and the national (racial) presuppositions when he said the issue was personal commitment. Surely if the Star of David could not be the Israelites' substitute, the Stars and Stripes cannot be ours either.

Then and now, we need to be reminded that there is a difference between being God's creation and being his child. We are all his creatures by virtue of our existence. We become his children by personal response, reception, and relationship. One birth of the physical nature for creaturehood. A second birth of the spiritual nature for childhood. How can we know which we are? One aspect of the test is to accept Jesus and what he says as coming from God himself. If we do, then we have

A FRESH START

God for our Father. If we do not, then we have another father. To a relativistic society, that sounds awfully cut and dried. But that's the way it is.

Lord, there are a lot of God-substitutes around today. Help me to never put my trust in them, but only in you through the life and words of Jesus. Amen.

DEATH

Scripture: John 8:48-59

Text: *If a man keeps my word, he will never see death (v. 51).*

Death. The mention of this word sends chills through many people. Psychologists tell us that whereas sex was the unmentionable subject of former generations, death is the unmentionable subject today.

I knew a person in seminary who was terrorized by a fear of death. Studies have revealed that many people enter the field of medicine because of that fear. The funeral business exists and thrives on the desire of people to put as much of a buffer zone between them and death as possible.

Into this confusion about death and the related hysteria, Jesus walks. He says if we keep his word, we will never taste death.

Is Jesus saying that the believer will not die at all? No. In the Greek, the key is in the word "taste" (v. 51, KJV). Although our bodies will return to the dust, we will not "taste" death if we are Christians. The Bible teaches that the natural, unavoidable cessation of life is not death. Rather, death is the negative, ultimate, and eternal experience of the spirit separated from God. Jesus is simply saying that if we keep his word, even though we expire physically, we will never die in the eternal sense of the word. This is in line with what Jesus said later, "He who believes in me will live [eternally and spiritually], even though he dies [physically]" (11:25). For millions, this is a great promise and hope. It is a liberation from great fear.

Dear God, I have some natural and normal anxiety about the end of my physical life and the lives of my loved ones. I would like to know how we'll die—when and where. But the real question and fears are about what happens after death. Thank you that you have given me some answers and grounds for hope. Thank you that the fear of death can be eliminated from my experience because I am a Christian. Thank you that because of Jesus' resurrection, the end of life here is just the beginning of life with you. Amen.

IT MATTERS WHERE YOU ARE

Scripture: John 9:1-12

Text: *Others said, "No, he only looks like him." But he himself insisted, "I am the man" (v. 9).*

Notice the contrast between the neighbors and the sight-restored man. The neighbors were quite sure he was not the same man who lived with them. They confessed that he looked like the blind beggar, but they could not bring themselves to admit it was he—even in the face of the man's own testimony. What does this say?

First, a person's perspective matters. If you are on the outside of Christianity looking in, your response will be far different than if you are on the inside looking out. The man, now looking through once-sightless eyes, was confident and matter-of-fact in his response. But the people observing from the outside were full of excuses and reasons not to believe.

It is still so today. Do not be discouraged by people in the world who do not see life as you do. Remember their perspective. Those on the outside of personal faith looking in have always been hard to convince. On the other hand, remember where you are and what has happened in your life. To those who have looked from the inside out, it has always been a matter of praise and confidence to say, "I once was blind, but now I see."

Second, don't let your personal experience sag because of someone else's secondhand observation. The man who had been healed didn't, and we must not either. The truth of Christianity is confirmed by those who live it, not those who observe it. You can listen all day to observers who give a hundred reasons why Christianity will not work. But how do they know? They haven't tried it. By contrast, millions of people all over the world, in all sorts of conditions, testify that it does work. They know because they have put Christianity to the test in the crucible of life and found it sufficient.

Remember, your perspective matters. It matters whether you are one who has had your eyes opened by Jesus or whether you are just an observer. What you see will be different. Don't be discouraged by those people who are merely looking on. Do what the healed man did—keep on insisting, insisting on the basis of what you *know* has happened to you.

Lord, it breaks my heart to hear people give the reasons they have for why Christianity won't work. But Lord, I know what you've done for my eyes—for my life. Help me today not to argue, but just proclaim and live. Amen.

JUST THE ANSWERS THAT COUNT

Scripture: John 9:13-34

Text: *One thing I do know. I was blind but now I see! (v. 25).*

It used to bother me when I got involved in religious discussions (which usually turned into arguments) with non-Christian dorm mates in college. I got upset because they threw questions at me I couldn't answer: What about the heathens who never hear of Christ? Why does God allow retardation? Where did Cain get his wife? What really got me was that when I couldn't come up with some snappy answer, they gloried in my defeat. Their idea of Christianity was that it had to have an airtight, on-the-spot answer for everything. And when it didn't, they claimed they had won and I had lost.

Praise God, today I have outgrown that false understanding of Christianity—indeed, of religion and philosophy in general. If I had only realized that the rules they were playing by were unrealistic, I would have saved myself much embarrassment and frustration. I now see the standards of perfection they tried to impose on me are not imposed on anyone or anything else. They certainly did not impose it on their homemade concoction of religion, or on the imperfect way they lived by their rules. They did not impose it on the science they studied, for the chemistry majors did not ridicule their professors or their lab work because they had some unanswered questions. The social theorists did not abandon their social concepts that didn't apply in all cases. But at the time I didn't see that. I only felt the pain of knowing what I knew, and felt helpless without all the answers.

Perhaps I can save you some needless worry and frustration. Christianity does not have all the answers—just the ones that

85

count. Don't get discouraged. No person or system of thought has them all. It is a matter of degree, and the degree makes the difference. In Christianity we have the highest degree of revelation concerning the nature of God, eternal life, and salvation. We have the highest degree of understanding how our imperfections are atoned for. We have the highest degree of relationship possible with an infinite God.

There are some things we do not know about Christ and the Christian faith, and non-Christians delight in confronting us with those very things. But they don't know either! However, no one can argue against one thing—your personal experience. No one can deny that and be fair. No one has the right to negate what has happened in your life.

The people who argued about the blind man had all the reasons for why he could not have his sight. They had the unanswerable questions and they threw them at the man, until he finally said, "I don't know everything, but I do know one thing. I used to be blind and now I can see. I do know that."

And that silenced them. It didn't convert them. But they had to cease their tactics in the face of once-blinded eyes, now seeing. When you witness from the stance of personal experience, people may still not accept what you say, but they will have to deal with it. They may conclude you are insane and go on trying to make Christianity conform to standards they would never accept for themselves. But come to think of it, they thought Jesus was mad too.

Lord, help me to see that you have not called me to win arguments but to live the life and proclaim the truth of what you have done and are doing in my life. Amen.

LORD, I BELIEVE

Scripture: John 9:35-41

Text: *"Lord, I believe," and he worshiped him (v. 38).*

Jesus knew this man had been through a pretty rough time, so he found him. For me, this is the most moving part of the whole account. Jesus comes to a man who has been under the gun and reconfirms the truth to him.

Haven't we all had those times when we've had it rough? Our faith has been raked over the coals and, although we made it through, in all honesty we have come out a little tired and the worse for wear.

The glorious truth is that God knows when this happens to us, and he cares! It is his nature to find us shortly thereafter and reconfirm the truth to us. It is his nature to take us in his arms like a loving Father and reinstill in us that full faith—maybe even fuller!

It may happen on a Sunday morning or evening worship. You have had a tough week. You have fought some spiritual battles. And then he meets you and lifts you up with renewed faith. It may come as you sit quietly today and read the Word, a devotional piece, or listen to music. It may come through a small group that God uses to minister to you. But God is there. You believe. And you worship him.

If the account of the blind man did not end this way, and if God didn't work in the experiences of life this way, I don't know how many defeats I could take before I would be crushed. But God is faithful! He comes to me when I am weary in well-doing. He thanks me for the fact that I have hung in there. And then he breaks the flask of spiritual renewal and pours it on my tired spirit—renewing me and letting me know that I have come through one more experience victorious. Yes, Lord, I believe. I worship you.

A FRESH START

Thank you, God, that you know just when to come around. I don't know what I would do without those meetings. I believe. Amen.

ENTERING AT THE DOOR

Scripture: John 10:1-6

Text: *The man who does not enter the sheep pen by the gate, but climbs in by some other way, is a thief and a robber (v. 1).*

The first twenty-one verses of chapter 10 have been some of the most beautiful and meaningful for me in my Christian growth, and I trust they can be the same for you. Read Psalm 23 with these verses. You will find a marvelous parallel between them, for they both describe the intensive shepherd-sheep relationship. From that relationship we can learn many lessons about the kind of relationship we can have with God through Jesus Christ.

This section begins with an emphasis upon entering at the gate. I remember coming home with my wife from an evangelistic meeting after driving long into the night because we wanted to get home so badly. Our baby son was asleep on the back seat. When we drove into the driveway and got ready to go in the house, we discovered we had left the house key inside. The next half hour was spent trying to find a window that might not be locked. At last we found it. But not before I had scuffed my shoes and ruined some clothes. During that experience I wished a thousand times for the key. How much easier it would have been if I had not forgotten it.

Jesus says the way to God is through the door, but many people simply will not accept that fact. They try to invent other means to the same end, and they get dirty, ruined, or scuffed up in the process. How much easier if they only would go in at the door.

The sheepfold is constructed especially with sheep in mind. Because sheep have a tendency to wander, there is only one door. Any sheep coming in or going out must pass through that door, and the shepherd sleeps in the doorway. We do not criticize the sheepfold for being built that way; it has been planned for the good of the sheep.

God's plan for the salvation of men is constructed and set up in a certain way. The irony is that while we accept the construction of a sheepfold, we find fault with the construction of the plan of salvation. It has a door too; but rather than use it, millions are trying to make their own doors and climb in by other ways.

There is one major difference between what such people do and what I did in my attempt that night. Whereas I made it inside, Jesus makes it plain that to try to climb in by any other means than the door is to fail. In our personal spiritual growth it is imperative that we use the door. Jesus says plainly, "I am the gate for the sheep" (v. 7). He is the door!

Dear Lord, I've had my share of scuffs and scrapes trying to get to you by other ways than the door. Thank you that one day in my frustrating scrambling around I spied the door and discovered through Jesus how to have a relationship with you. Help me show the door to others. Amen.

THE LIFE-GIVER

Scripture: John 10: 7-10

Text: *I have come that they may have life, and have it to the full (v. 10).*

Jesus is the door through which we pass into a meaningful relationship with God. When we pass through that door, we discover an entirely new dimension to life.

One of the greatest discoveries I have made in my study of God's Word and in my Christian life is that there is a difference between being alive and living. Every person on the face of this earth is alive, but not everyone is living. When Jesus came, he made this necessary distinction, a distinction between mere physical life and the abundant life that affects the whole man.

When Jesus said, "I have come that they may have life," he was speaking to a group of people who were alive. And yet, he dared to offer them life. What's the lesson? Again, it is one thing to be alive and another thing to be living—abundantly.

A shepherd's function was to give the sheep life. Oh, they were alive when he first began to work with them, but they would not remain so for very long without his help. In order that they would not eat something that would kill them, the shepherd would go along the route they would travel and burn off every harmful plant he could find.

The sheep would tend to wander from the rest of the flock and fall over a cliff to their death, or become stuck in a crevice. So the shepherd planned the route from the lowlands to the highlands, steering clear of the cliffs as much as possible. Then he carried a staff that he could use to retrieve stuck sheep.

The shepherd planned a route that went past green pastures and by still waters, where the thirsty and tired sheep could be refreshed. As far as the sheep were concerned, the shepherd was their life-giver.

Jesus comes to us in precisely the same way and makes the

same offer. We too have a journey to make, and without him we can never make it. He comes to offer us a dimension of experience, help, and encouragement that can only be called "abundant life." If it is abundant, I can use all I need and never use it up!

The secret is discovering the distinction between being alive and living. Many never see the difference, so they limp through life. I trust you have made the distinction. Today look to Christ, your shepherd, as your life-giver. Draw from his resources. Depend on him as your source.

Lord, for too long I saw no difference between being alive and living. Thank you for the day I saw the distinction and asked you to give me abundant life. Help me today to utilize that life. Amen.

THROUGH THICK AND THIN

Scripture: John 10:11-13

Text: *The good shepherd lays down his life for the sheep (v. 11).*

The testimony of the saints throughout the ages has been that Christ was with them through thick and thin. Paul, imprisoned and facing death wrote, "I have learned, in whatsoever state I am, . . . to be content" (Phil. 4:11, KJV). The source of his contentment? The assurance that God was with him. Stephen, the first Christian martyr, died with forgiveness on his lips. Why? Because God was with him. John Wesley's final words were "Best of all, God is with us." Corrie Ten Boom walked through human hell and made it, because God was with her. A sick saint in the rest home greets you each time you visit her with "Isn't Jesus wonderful?" Why? Because he *is* with her moment by moment. A sinner rises from his knees, forgiven. Why? Because Jesus, the good shepherd, had laid down his life for him.

And that's the ultimate! We see evidence of the reality of the Christian faith and the utter dependability of Jesus Christ in times of tragedy and despair. If Christianity is only for the "spiritual highs," then it is not worth having. Life has too many lows. If Jesus is only with us in the sunshine, that's not sufficient. There are too many shadows. But if he is there—always—that's different!

To what extent is Christ willing to go for you and me? To death. I read the story of a shepherd who was attacked by robbers who wanted to steal his sheep. The shepherd literally fought the robbers until he died. He gave up his life trying to defend the sheep against harm and danger. Only love would do that.

Who would you die for? Make a list. When you have made it,

you will find it contains the names of those you love most dearly. What does that tell you about Jesus when he says he has laid down his life for *you?* Charles Wesley put the words and the music together and captured it in a great hymn:

> Amazing love, how can it be
> That Thou, my God, shouldst die for me?

Live your Christian life today in the glorious assurance and joy that Jesus is with you through thick and thin. Why? Because he loves you!

Jesus, you are here with me right now. Today may be sunshine. Or shadow. Or both. But with you I'm ready to live it. Amen.

KNOWLEDGE AND KNOWING

Scripture: John 10:14-21

Text: *I know my sheep and my sheep know me (v. 14).*

Just as there is a difference between being alive and living, there is also a difference between knowledge and knowing. If we are to grow as Christians and be effective in our discipleship, this distinction is crucial. It is one thing to know *about* Jesus; it is another thing to *know* him.

Let's begin with the word *know.* In the Greek language it is translated from a word that means "knowledge based on relationship." Bullinger's *Critical Lexicon and Concordance* says, "It denotes a personal and true relation between the person knowing and the object known." This is not strict intellectual knowledge, but rather knowledge derived by experience. We could paraphrase this verse by saying, "I know my own because I am in relationship with them, and my sheep know me because they are in relationship with me." The true disciple is one who not only knows about Jesus but also knows him through relationship.

The distinction is easily seen when applied to life. Suppose I were to tell you many things about the President: facts about his early life, his political career, his major accomplishments. I might know more about the President than anyone else. But if you asked me, "Have you ever met the President? Have you ever walked with him? Have you spent time with him in the White House?", I would have to answer, "No."

Your response would probably be, "Then you don't really know him, do you?" And the case would be closed.

It is essential that we see the difference between factual knowledge and knowing based on relationship. This is the key problem in many church-related colleges and seminaries. Students equate their professors' Ph.D.'s and knowledge about God with personal knowledge based on relationship. It is a crucial problem in many local churches in which members assume that worshiping and sitting under Christian teaching equal Christianity. It is a vital problem in our personal lives; we may be deceived into believing the things we know about Jesus mean we know him personally.

Many play down the importance of relationship. And perhaps we could too if it were not for one thing. Jesus said, "I know my sheep and my sheep know me." That's *relationship*.

Today the important issue to be settled in our lives is relationship. Discipleship requires it. Christian growth requires it. And we can't be satisfied very long without it.

Thank you, God, that I can know you—not just know about you. Amen.

HE DID TELL US

Scripture: John 10:22-42

Text: *I did tell you, but you do not believe (v.25).*

The Jews didn't want to know who Jesus was. When he told them, they didn't believe. Instead, they tried to kill him.

The intriguing thing in this passage is the bluntness of the request: "Tell us *plainly*" (v.24). We can assume that when Jesus said, "I did tell you," he meant, "I have told you *plainly*."

What is the plain answer Jesus gave? The passage reveals at least three clear indications of who he was.

First, the *miracles* of Jesus attest to his Messiahship. Jesus is saying, "Look at what I have done and am doing; this is the most visible proof of who I am." He gave the same answer to those whom John the Baptist sent to inquire about him. Jesus told the messengers to tell John that the blind saw, the deaf heard, the lame walked, the dead were raised, and the gospel was being proclaimed. These activities would be sufficient to convince the Jews.

As a young man in college, Lew Wallace set out to write a book to expose Christianity for the hoax he felt it was. He decided to read the Gospels, find the weaknesses, and expose them. But before he finished, he had been converted. The weight of the evidence was conclusive and confirming. Instead of his exposé, he wrote the classic *Ben Hur*.

Jesus is saying, "The evidence is conclusive. Look at the miracles." Did Jesus tell us plainly who he was? The Scripture says, "Yes, through the miracles."

A second verification was in the *man*. Notice how Jesus is moving from the outside in. He begins with the miracles. Now he points to himself and says, "I and the Father are one" (v. 30), appealing to his unique nature. The Jews immediately picked this up and accused him of blasphemy in claiming equality with God. But Jesus was only doing what they had asked him to do—tell them plainly.

It is not enough merely to say you are someone. Some people in institutions today say they are Napoleon, and others even claim to be Christ. You can *say* you are anyone, but that does not automatically make it so. It is here that the man and the miracle come together. The pitifully insane say they are Jesus but do not convince anyone. They do not walk on the water, heal the sick, or raise the dead. But Jesus claims to be one with the Father—and then does the things only God could do. The miracles and the man confirm each other. As Nicodemus said earlier in this Gospel, "No one could perform the miraculous signs you are doing if God were not with him" (3:2). He did tell us.

The third verification, which is more intangible, is the *mission*. Jesus said the Father had set him apart as his very own and sent him into the world. He was a unique man, doing unique things, because he was on a unique mission. If God the Father could send forth his Son into the world, then it is not illogical and inconsistent to believe that such a person would be unlike anyone else.

In order of time, Jesus has reversed the proofs. In time, the mission was first, then the man, then the miracles. But Jesus is trying to take us from that which should be the most obvious and compelling to that which is before time and at the very heart of the eternal God.

Has the absolute power of this passage gripped you today? The Jews missed the message because their preconceptions made it impossible for them to see even in the face of the evidence. With your fresh start, I trust that is not your problem. I hope your vision is clear and your sight is keen so you will see that he did tell us in no uncertain terms that he was the Christ through his miracles, his manhood, and his mission.

Thank you, Jesus, for telling us plainly who you are. I know you are the same yesterday, today, and forever. You are the Christ today. You are Lord right now. As I live today, let me experience your lordship. Amen.

LOVE IN DETAIL

Scripture: John 11:1-16

Text: *Jesus loved Martha and her sister and Lazarus (v. 5).*

Many high-water marks are in the Gospel of John. The story of the death of Lazarus is one. People have turned to it again and again for a word from God.

The first message from this story is that God does not love in generalities. He loves in specifics. He does not just blanket the world with his love; he directs it into the hearts of individuals. John does not say that Jesus loved "this family," although we know he did. Instead, we see that Jesus had a special love for each of the family members. As we discover why this was so, we shall also learn why he feels the same toward us.

First, Martha, Mary, and Lazarus were all unique creations of God. No collective love would fit them all. Jesus had met them and known them as individuals, and he loved them that way. As you and I live out this day, we can know we are not lost in the mass of humanity. Jesus loves each of us. Why? Because you and I are unique among all the creations of God. Line up every person who has ever lived, who is alive now, and who will live; march them by you, and you will never see yourself! He loves each of us because we are one of a kind.

Second, Jesus expressed his love individually because their needs were different, and he was aware of the differences. Only love that fits the need would suffice in the darkest hour.

I first heard this truth in a sermon recorded by Charles L. Allen, a well-known Methodist preacher. Go back and look at the words of our text. Repeat them slowly. Pause between each name. Then repeat them slowly again. Only this time when you finish the last name, add your own.

Amazing, but true. Jesus loves you!

The theologian Karl Barth was asked near the end of his life to put into words the greatest theological thought he had ever known. His reply was "Jesus loves me; this I know, for the Bible tells me so."

Sing that song quietly to yourself. It is not a children's song at all; it is the greatest song in the world. It speaks in detail of love—the only kind of love God knows anything about, and the only kind of love Jesus ever expresses.

God, it is so easy for me to get the feeling that I am lost in the crowd, that no one cares about me, that no one cares if I am alive. But today you have revealed to me so clearly that you know and care. As I go through this day, help me to pause often and remember that you love me with a love so special that it could only fit my life. Thank you for that love. Help me to know that the only person in the world who can love you the way I can, is me. Amen.

MARTHA—THE ACTIVIST

Scripture: John 11:17-37

Text: *When Martha heard that Jesus was coming, she went out to meet him (v. 20).*

The love and ministry of Jesus were tailored to the needs of each person caught up in the grief-laden situation over Lazarus's death. We begin with Martha and her needs because she is the one with whom John begins.

It is not easy to calculate the precise time that had elapsed. If we take the two days mentioned in verse 6 and include them in the four days Lazarus had lain in the tomb, then four days had passed. If we add the two sets of days, nearly a week had transpired since Jesus first heard of the death of his friend. Either way, it was a long time. The Jewish grieving process was well under way. But when Martha heard that Jesus was coming at last, she jumped to her feet and ran to meet him.

Martha was reacting typically, for her. Do you recall the account in Luke 10:38-42 when Jesus visited in the home of Mary and Martha? (If you do not, take time now to turn there and read it.) Martha was busy getting things in order, while Mary sat quietly at the feet of Jesus and listened to his teaching. Something in the personality of Martha wanted to get with it. She would be the one today who is always saying, "Let's get this show on the road"; or "Quit holding up things; let's get going." If there was something that needed doing, Martha wanted to dive in and get it done. How did Jesus love her? And in loving her, how did he minister to her?

The problem with Martha and all who are like her is that in their activity they run the risk of losing sight of the priorities. In their desire to do something, there is a chance they might do the wrong thing. Martha, the activist, needed to be made aware of the issues. So when Martha met Jesus with her "let's get on with it" attitude, his response was not one of action, but

101

of perspective. Jesus loved Martha and ministered to her by calling her attention to himself.

And that is what she needed. The real issue was not Lazarus's death. Everyone has to die, even Lazarus. The issue was not to be resolved by some form of hurried activity. Instead, it was to be resolved in recognizing who Jesus was and what power he had. So instead of doing anything quickly, Jesus first laid the foundation.

The principal for those of us who are activists is plain. We must know where to direct our activity and how to direct it, or we may go off half-cocked. We must know why we are active, or we won't learn anything from our activity.

Martha was in danger of missing the real purpose in what was about to happen because of her desire to get with it. She would have been tempted to act without thinking, get Lazarus back, go on to some other need, and miss the impact of the whole thing. Jesus slowed her down and showed her what it was all about. Then her concern for action and his willingness to act accomplished a purpose.

As growing Christians, we can see so much that needs doing. But we must never get so busy doing things that we forget why we are doing them. In Chaucer's *Canterbury Tales*, the parson is said to always have been busy, but no one ever knew what he was busy about. That's the danger of us Marthas. Jesus ministers to us by getting us to see first what the real issues are and why he wants us to be involved. Today, instead of getting with it, we need to get with *Him*.

You have taught me today, God, through Martha. Slow me down too. Let me see you first; then I can know why I act, how I act, where I act, and when I act. Save me from activity that is no longer staked down to priorities. Amen.

MARY—THE MYSTIC

Scripture: John 11:17-37

Text: *But Mary stayed at home (v. 20).*

Labels are always inadequate. If we try to characterize Martha, Mary, and Lazarus with one word, we will leave out some things. For example, whereas Martha was the activist, Mary was the mystic.

Two other Scripture passages also indicate Mary's thoughtful nature. The first is Luke 10, in which Mary sits at the Lord's feet and listens to his teachings while Martha works to make everything just right. The second passage is the one John reminds his readers about in 11:2, recorded in Matthew 26:6-13 and Luke 7:36-50. (If you do not know the story of Mary's anointing Jesus' feet with perfume, take time now to read it.) In both stories, Mary assumes a more mystical role. If Martha runs the risk of getting so busy that she misses the real point, Mary risks getting so turned in on herself that nothing else gets done.

Note that when she finally does come to Jesus, he does not discourse with her in the same way that he did with Martha. Instead, he moves to action by saying, "Where have you laid him?" (John 11:34). He shakes Mary out of her more passive, lethargic spirit and calls her to act with him.

There are personality types today like Mary, who always want to muse on the latest spiritual truth. In times of tragedy they turn inward, perhaps to draw on that inner living water, but sometimes to retreat from life. While Jesus is grateful for the fact that we turn to inner resources to meet outer pressures, he will not let us stop living in the process. He calls such persons to action—to go on living.

The awesome beauty of this passage is that through the loving ministry of Jesus, he brings Mary and Martha to the same place. Martha, the doer, is brought to the place where her action makes sense. Mary, the thinker, is brought to the place where her sense becomes action. And miracles happen.

I am sure there is much more here, and it may be that you will want to spend some extra time thinking about these two women and how Jesus ministered his unique love to them. Lessons learned here will help us to know better how he will minister uniquely to us and our personalities.

Dear God, thank you that you will not let me withdraw into a shell, even if I am contemplating good, spiritual things. Thank you for reminding me lovingly that I must take my good theology, right doctrine, and holy thinking and put them to work on that which is dead and dying in me and around me. Amen.

LAZARUS—THE DEAD MAN

Scripture: John 11: 33-44

Text: *Where have you laid him? (v. 34).*

The third major figure in the Lazarus incident is Lazarus himself. We have seen how Jesus dealt with Martha and Mary and brought them to a place of joining with him in meeting the need of his friend. As we come to this point in the story we are on familiar ground, for all of us have been "dead in trespasses and sins," and even now we continue to discover putrifying areas within ourselves. We are Lazarus. In seeing how Jesus ministers to him, we can gain insight into our need.

First, the important thing to see is that Lazarus is not the focus. We have already pointed out that Jesus was not really saving Lazarus from death for eventually Lazarus would have to die, just as every person does. The real focus is on the glory of God. This will help us to remember that we are not the focus either. We get too self-centered in our witness. While it is tremendous to know "I once was blind, but now I see," we must always remember that the reason for the miracle goes beyond our personal benefit. The ultimate purpose is to glorify God, who desires that our new life will stand before dying men of the world and say, "God did this! He can do it for you, too."

Second, we learn that Jesus seeks out death. He takes the initiative by asking, "Where is he?" This was the first question God asked after Adam and Eve sinned—"Where are you?" From the first pages of Scripture to the last, we continue to meet a God who seeks us out in our sin and death. He comes to us in our tombs. In our Christian growth, we should never get the idea that we must somehow get to God with works, pleasing character, or impeccable integrity. No! The fact is that God is seeking us. He wants to go to the areas of our lives where death still has its hold.

Third, death makes Jesus cry. "Jesus wept" (v. 35), the

shortest verse in Scripture, speaks volumes on the nature of God. Whenever there is death, God's heart is broken. Some say God *sends* people to hell. Don't you believe it! God never sends anyone to hell; he only allows them to go where they are already headed. God is not willing that any should perish, and in the presence of death, his heart is broken. Look at the cross, and you will see the extent to which God has gone in order to turn all men back to himself and rescue them out of their tombs of death. If anyone walks out of God's presence into eternal separation and looks back, he will not see a God who says, "That's all for you," but rather a God who weeps.

Fourth, Jesus removes the stone. He does for us what we cannot do for ourselves. We stand powerless in the face of sin. It is impossible for us to get the obstacles out of the way. We cannot clear the path between life and death. But he can. And he does! What stones are in your life today? Listen, he is speaking: "Take away the stone" (v. 39).

Fifth, Jesus calls us to move out. When, by his power, he has done for us what we cannot do for ourselves, he then calls us to do what we can—move closer to him in a faith-response of our whole life. He calls us by name. He tells us to move. Don't stay in the tomb. Walk out. The way of freedom is there.

Sixth, Jesus unravels the graveclothes. I do not want to read too much symbolism into this passage, but I do think there is a message here for us. Even when the stone is rolled away, and even when I have been called out, and even when I have stumbled and staggered from death into life, there is still a lot of unwrapping that needs to be done. The light and life expose further "stripping off the old man" that I need to do. Jesus saw this. Lazarus was out of the tomb. He was alive. But he was not totally free. To have left him like that would have been to have left him in misery. So Jesus immediately initiated the unraveling process.

He does the same for us; and that process goes on until we reach perfection. It is then that Jesus finally says, "Let him go" (v. 44). The words of liberation and freedom! We need to hear them, and Jesus speaks them to us as well.

As you live today, listen. Some stones are rolling away in

your life in the master's presence.

Thank you, Jesus, for not turning away from the death in my life. Thank you for dealing with it. In some areas of my life I am out of the tomb. Continue the unraveling process in me today until I am wholly yours. Amen.

STAY IN YOUR PLACE

Scripture: John 11:45-57

Text: *So from that day on they plotted to take his life (v. 53).*

People could tolerate Jesus as long as he stayed in his place and played the role of the itinerant preacher. Israel had had its share of roving preachers and prophets. They had built up an immunity to them.

But Jesus was different. His growing influence was becoming a threat to the religious and political structures, and when that happened, he had to go. The high priest tried to make it sound so patriotic by saying, "Better for you that one man die for the people than that the whole nation perish" (v. 50). But the truth was, the religionists were threatened by Jesus. So from that day on they plotted to take his life.

A similar line of thought in our time says that religion is all right as long as it stays in its place. Christianity is respectable, even popular in some places, but we don't want it to get out of hand. Even today, when the church attempts to speak out against social evils or corrupt structures, it receives criticism from some, sometimes even from so-called good church people who think the church ought to stay out of that sort of thing and "just preach the Gospel."

Jesus reminds us in this passage that any faith that does not penetrate into real, everyday living is no faith at all. A gospel reserved only for Sunday and stained glass is tainted. So Jesus did not stay in his place—he took on the church of his day and called it to task for its hypocrisy and compromise. He challenged the nation and its leaders, who had abandoned true faith in God for the favor of Caesar.

Jesus still does the same thing today; he still challenges phoniness wherever it exists. A church that dares to declare the gospel in society is no embarrassment to Jesus. What embarrasses him is the church that condones the way of the world and tries to put God's approval upon it.

As we grow in our faith, we must learn that authentic faith acts in life and reacts to life. To be sure, there is a difference between being obnoxious and being committed. Some well-meaning Christians may need to learn that difference. But most of us simply need to remember that any area of life is fair game for the application of gospel principles. When certain segments of society try to keep religion in its place, the disciple will respond with John Wesley's words, "The world is my parish." We may experience some financial loss from living out this position, but the truth generated will be a hundred times greater than if we tried to stay in our place.

Dear God, help me to remember that my place as a Christian is anywhere and everywhere. Help me to remember that no society, institution, or structure is above your judgment. Help me to reflect a quality of life and commitment that will not compromise in the face of anything that is wrong. It may cost me something. It did Jesus. Grant me the strength of faith to be willing to pay that price for your glory and his. In Jesus' name. Amen.

CONSISTENCY

Scripture: John 12:1-11

Text: *Why wasn't this perfume sold and the money given to the poor?
. . . [Judas] did not say this because he cared about the poor but
because he was a thief; as a keeper of the money bag, he used to
help himself to what was put into it (vv. 5, 6).*

Jesus had returned to Bethany and to the home of Mary,
Martha, and Lazarus. During the course of dinner, Mary took
perfume and anointed Jesus' feet. This threw Judas Iscariot
into a rage, apparently for worthwhile reasons. But John
makes it clear that Judas's surface philanthropy was just a
smoke screen.

Words have always been used to cover up truth. Today,
politicians can choose their words and tell us nothing while
claiming to tell us everything. Contracts can be worded so as to
make their meaning vague. Advertisements can be worded
with hidden meaning and appeal. Church resolutions can be
worded with authority and dismissed casually.

Our generation has come close to mastering the art of word
games. Political leaders can sit before television cameras in a
Senate hearing and declare their innocence, and later, in a
trial, be found guilty. Government agencies can deny they
have been involved in citizens' lives, while a closer examina-
tion reveals their lie. Business and industry can highlight the
"American way" in the economic world, only to be found
exploiting and cheating workers and clients. Churches can
advocate something as noble as the gospel and, at the same
time, be involved in questionable activities. The Judas-
syndrome lives on.

All this should evidence the necessity for consistency between our outer professions and our inner living. A restoration
of this consistency could renew the greatness of our nation. A
loss of it may eat away our foundations and future, both

individually and corporately.

We need a fresh start in consistency today. As we grow in our faith, it is important that our words and our lives match up. It is the only way to prevent becoming religious schizophrenics. It is the only way that unreached people will be drawn to the Christian faith.

Heavenly Father, I am already too aware of times when my words and my life fail to match up. I see many examples around me in which words are intentionally used to cover up what is really going on. By the power of your Spirit, help me never to cover up my life with my words. Let there be consistency between my believing and living. Let my mouth report what is going on in my heart. Amen.

BEWARE OF THE CROWD

Scripture: John 12:12-19

Text: *The great crowd that had come for the Feast . . . took palm branches and went out to meet him, shouting (vv. 12, 13).*

If you imagine a Hollywood movie scene of this event, it will not take you long to get caught up in it. We have traditionally called this the "triumphal entry," and it was indeed! The welcome Jesus received was unparalleled in the history of Jerusalem. It was a welcome for a king, a conqueror, a hero. And the people made sure that it had all the sights and sounds worthy of such an event. There may have been as many as two and a half million people. No wonder the Pharisees said, "The whole world has gone after him!" (v. 19).

But beware of the crowd! It is so fickle. This event took place just a week before Jesus was condemned to die, again by the crowd. Quite likely some in the crucifixion crowd had been in the hosanna crowd a week earlier. It seems inconceivable that people's emotions could change so quickly, but they did.

The same thing happens today. A group of several hundred young people gets really caught up in the excitement of a spiritual experience; several months later they are back to normal in their youth groups at home. A congregation of several hundred members really gets turned on by a renewal weekend; later we find out that some members are suing each other and the church is split down the middle. A large city has a huge evangelistic crusade. Thousands make decisions. Later many are never heard from again as counselors try to follow them up.

What is happening? It is the problem of getting caught up in the tidal wave of the crowd. Some people, because of their personalities, are easily carried along by the high tides of crowd experiences. They see a lot of people really getting turned on, and they go along for the ride. But when the event

112

that sustained the crowd's enthusiasm is over, these people have nothing to motivate them to further growth in their faith.

Is this to say that Christians should avoid such activities? Some believe so. Some well-meaning pastors and laypersons refuse to support community evangelistic efforts because of all that emotionalism. Others discourage people from participating in special events because "it won't last."

Let's set the record straight. It is not the fault of the events, but of the people. Too many times we fail to look beyond the event to what it is trying to accomplish. We get carried away by the music of the rock concert, and forget that the performers are singing about Jesus and trying to get us to know him better.

In our spiritual lives, we need to beware of the crowd. That does not mean we have to avoid the crowd; rather, we need to look deeper than many in the crowd look. We need to look to the real message and purpose that bring the crowd together. Look to Jesus. Commit ourselves to him. That way, when the stadium is dark, when the rock group has gone on to another show, when the evangelist has gone on to the next meeting, when the camp is over, we will still have someone to cling to—Jesus. He will not have moved on.

Lord, I get caught up in the crowd. I enjoy the life of the crowd because sometimes it stands in contrast to the quiet boredom I see around me. But let me know that where there is a crowd, there is a reason for it. Let me look for that reason, find it, and commit myself to that—not to the crowd. Amen.

TRUE GLORIFICATION

Scripture: John 12:20-36

Text: *The hour has come for the Son of Man to be glorified (v. 23).*

Everything that happens in the remainder of this gospel occurred in the last week in Jesus' life. The fact that John devotes nearly half of his Gospel to the last seven days of the life of Christ is a significant clue to the importance of what follows. Jesus' hour had come.

In this hour he began to speak about glorification. He compared it to a grain of wheat, saying that true glorification is similar to what happens to that grain. His glorification and ours will resemble that process.

There is a vast difference between what the world counts as glory and what Christ says it is. *Glory* in worldly terms is a star-spangled word. People shout, "Glory!" and you can hear the word snap, crackle, and pop. For a person to "get the glory" is for that person to stand tall in the limelight, to be hailed by his fellowmen, to get the credit. In the world, *glory* stands for accomplishment, reward, and success. But in the realm of discipleship and God's Kingdom, true glory comes in other ways and consists of other things.

First of all, glory comes not through achieving, but through giving. The kernel of wheat has to give itself in order for the glory to come. Selfishness has to go. Doing your thing must yield to doing God's thing. The real honor comes not in getting but in giving. Our world has been blessed by those people who have caught the truth of this passage and gone on to pattern their lives after it. Our lives will make an impact if we will remember and practice this truth.

Second, true glory comes not in standing out, but in putting out. The idea is related to what has just been said, but here I am thinking about the fact that real greatness is not measured by being hailed as the one who never needed anyone else. Glory is not for the one who wants to stand on the pedestal. Instead, glory comes in being willing to do your work quietly. The kernel is buried, out of sight, and it is there that it does its real work. Some people slack off when they are not in the center of things, but those who are truly great work equally hard in the shadows or the sunlight.

Third, true glory comes not from success but from sacrifice. We cannot ignore the fact that what Jesus says here is said in life and death categories. We must divorce glory from its American and Western connotations. We say that to have glory you've got to succeed, you've got to make it. Jesus says that the greatest person is the person who serves sacrificially. He did. Glory will come to us if we follow his example.

The hour had come for Jesus to participate in the glory that he had been moving toward. And that glory involved a cross. Our hour has come in the life of faith to see what true glory is all about. We will miss it if we seek it the way the world does. We will find it if we look for it in such things as giving, working, and sacrificing.

Lord, let me glorify you today. Not by saying, "Look what a great guy I am," but rather, "Look what a great Savior I have." Amen.

LIKE FATHER, LIKE SON

Scripture: John 12: 37-50

Text: *When a man believes in me, he does not believe in me only, but in the one who sent me (v. 44).*

An important, recurring theme in the Gospel of John is that of the close relationship between Jesus and the Father. On more than one occasion Jesus made it clear that, because of this relationship, we cannot accept the Father without accepting the Son, and that to reject the Son is also to reject the Father. He said plainly, "I and the Father are one" (10: 30). This statement has many implications for our contemporary situation.

For one thing, it is a blow against cultural religion. People in every generation have always been religious. Atheists are extremely rare. Nearly everyone believes in "God," as they understand the meaning of that word. But to believe in Jesus is something else again. We want to believe in a God who exists, but do not have to take him all that seriously if we confine him to the regions of heaven. When we see Jesus, however, we are confronted with a real person who claimed equality with God, who was incarnate, and who invaded real space and time.

If I do not want to be invaded, then I can try to reject Jesus while holding on to my belief in God. Much secular religion does this. We are quite willing to worship God, but far less willing to let Christ become Lord of our lives. This verse cuts through cultural Christianity and says we cannot have God and reject Jesus, for they are one and the same. If we don't take Jesus, then it is a direct refusal to accept God the Father, who is one in nature with Jesus, who sent him into the world, and who said, "This is my Son, whom I love. Listen to him!" (Mark 9: 7).

For another thing, it gives Jesus his rightful place in the divine order. Dr. James Kennedy, who has pioneered the Evangelism Explosion ministry, has said that in visiting with

116

people, he has found most of them quite willing to acknowledge Jesus as a great teacher or philosopher, as one of the greatest men who ever lived. But he says millions do not accept and others do not know that Jesus is the God-man.

Again, the reason is clear. If Jesus is only a wise man, then I can read what he has to say much as I read Plato, Shakespeare, or Confucius. But if Jesus is God become man, then I have to take him seriously. Every word. I have to believe he is alive in the world today, standing outside the hearts of men and desiring to enter. And that is something else. So I make a neat intellectual distinction. I accept the validity of his teaching without accepting the validity of his nature or the claims he made about himself.

But the Christian gospel is clear. We cannot separate the man from the message. We cannot separate the Son from the Father. To try is to attempt to break something that cannot be broken, and we will only become broken ourselves.

John is emphatic here and throughout this book. I am sure you have caught this before now, but today is a good time to ponder it for its own sake. Like Father like Son is nowhere more true than when we encounter Jesus. In him we have encountered the living God.

Heavenly Father, I cannot fully understand you because of your infinite nature. But thank you that in Jesus I see you and can know more about you than anywhere else in the world. Amen.

FOOT WASHING REVISITED

Scripture: John 13:1-17

Text: *Lord, are you going to wash my feet? (v. 6).*

By this event John says Jesus began to demonstrate the "full extent of his love" (v. 1). On the night before he went to the cross, Jesus began to teach the depth of discipleship. Today, let us look at what the foot washing meant for Peter.

It was the custom in Palestine for people's feet to be washed before they entered a house. When they visited friends, they would already have bathed; but after the dusty walk, they would need to have their feet sponged off before going into a home. The ritual of foot washing was the ritual of entry. It was an act of love and courtesy performed by the host. For the traveler, it was an act of submission to the ministry of his friend.

When Peter refused to allow Jesus to wash his feet, he was doing three things: refusing the ritual of entry, not accepting the ministry of his friend, and letting pride stand in the way. These things had to go before Jesus could count on him for effective service in the Kingdom.

The principle is clear for us. The significance of the foot washing is that we must let Jesus do something in us and to us. The person who will not submit to the ministry of Jesus in his life is not of the right spirit to be a disciple.

Jesus would soon be going away. His future ministry to the disciples would be through the Holy Spirit, a far less tangible agent than a basin and towel. If Peter would not submit to the physical ministry, he would never be able to submit to the spiritual ministry.

Peter finally caught on. When he realized the essential nature of what Jesus was doing, he said, "Not just my feet but my hands and my head as well!" (v. 9). What Peter meant was, "Lord, I don't want to miss anything you have for me. My whole being is yours to do with as you please." He was ready.

Are we ready? Have we put pride out of the way and taken the first step toward usefulness? Have we let Jesus do something in us and to us? If so, then Christ kneels and washes us.

Lord, I am so hesitant to let you minister to me. I try to do too much myself. I'm tired of all my running around. My feet are dusty. Please wash them. Amen.

WHO IS THE BETRAYER?

Scripture: John 13:18-30

Text: *He who shares my bread has lifted up his heel against me (v. 18).*

Today we examine a chilling truth as we get a glimpse into the nature of betrayal. It is easy to spot the betrayer who is openly defiant of Christ and his church, and thus far it has been easy to identify the hostility of Jesus' enemies in the Gospel. But betrayal also can occur in the company of those closest to Christ.

It is sobering to discover that one who observed Jesus so closely could have sold him so cheaply. But it happened! Christ's downfall came at the hands of one of his chosen disciples.

I was traveling with a group in India. Part of our journey included a week's stay in the ancient city of Bidar, an old Muslim fortress-city surrounded by a dry moat and high walls. Nearly five hundred years ago it was considered impenetrable, but the city fell. How? Not by powerful armies from without, but through bribery within. The gatekeeper was finally offered enough money to betray his own people. That's how Bidar fell, and I learned later that most of the fortress-cities in the area fell the same way.

In our own time we have heard politicians, sociologists, and military experts warn us that America is in more danger of collapse from within than from outward overthrow. History is full of examples supporting this warning.

The same warning must be leveled at the church. There are times when we appear to be betraying Christ by the things we do and the stands we take. Boards and agencies engage in questionable activities. Church funds are given to support causes offensive to the gospel. Some clergy do not really believe what they preach. Laymen do not live what they profess.

While we are pointing fingers at those who betray Christ with open defiance, let us not forget to include those who betray him while "sharing his bread." In our quest for authentic discipleship, we must remember the example of Judas. Even those closest to Christ are not beyond selling out for the right price.

In the final analysis, who is the betrayer? The person who openly rejects Christ and lets you know? Or the person who professes Christ and lives in opposition to his will? Keep watch on your soul; the tempter is at work in the inner circle too!

Lord, it is amazing how one of your own could betray you then—and now. Keep me so sensitive and open to your leading that I may faithfully live my faith. Amen.

THE REAL TEST

Scripture: John 13:31-38

Text: *All men will know that you are my disciples if you love one another (v. 35).*

Throughout Scripture, love is the test of our faith. God's love is the source of the gospel. Paul says love is the supreme quality. And here Jesus establishes the standard of love as the real test of discipleship. In a success-oriented society this seems strange. It may even be hard for some in the church to understand if they have thought the best Christians are the ones who have held the key offices the longest. Jesus reduces discipleship to the lowest common denominator: love. If we love one another, we and all men will know we are truly disciples.

The absence of this love is devastating. I still recall the day I was in one of the homes of my seminary parish. The wife was a church member; the husband was not. The wife was not home, the husband was. We began talking. Somewhere in the conversation he asked the dynamite question, "Preacher, why should I join that church, when the people who are in it can't even get along with each other?" All my theological defenses went up, and I mentally protected myself with all the catchy phrases about rationalizations and hypocrites. But then I realized that whether or not this man was using this as an excuse was not the point. He had made a vital observation. The absence of love had devastated the witness of the church to this man. Its absence devastates any church, anywhere.

The presence of love is invigorating. The telephone rang. It was a member asking me to visit a woman whose husband had cancer and was near death in a hospital hundreds of miles away. Except for a few friends, she was alone in her need, with no church and no pastor. I went to the home and got to know her. When her husband died, I preached his funeral. Shortly after his death, she appeared at the church one Sunday morning; not long after that, she wanted to join. I had been very careful in my previous visits not to mention joining the church, lest she think I only cared about her as a prospective member. So when she joined, I was curious as to her reason. She told me, "I want to be part of a church where people love each other like you all have loved me." The presence of caring love had redeemed her.

I could write at length about the churches that have died for lack of love. I could tell you even more about the churches that are vital because they have love.

If we are going to impress the world for Christ, we are not going to do it with big buildings and claims about our greatness. We are going to impress people by our love for one another and for them. That is the real test.

Father, forgive me for the times I have substituted secondary, man-made standards of spiritual success for the real standard: *love*. Fill me now with the presence of Christ, who is love. Amen.

TRUST IN THE SHADOWS

Scripture: John 14:1-4

Text: *Trust in God; trust also in me (v. 1).*

There are two kinds of athletes. Some play regardless of the weather. Others decide whether to participate on the basis of the forecast. This second group is called fair-weather athletes, and I confess I am one of them.

There are two kinds of Christians. Some express faith in God regardless of the situation. Others are high on Jesus when it's convenient and down on him when it's not. In psychology such persons are called manic-depressives, high one moment and low the next. We are not without our share of spiritual manic-depressives.

With John 14, we begin the most concentrated and significant teaching of our Lord. He was speaking on the night of his betrayal. It was just before his death and came just before he was to be separated from his disciples. It would not be long before his apostles would be exposed to their severest temptations.

Jesus began, "Trust in God; trust also in me." He knew the faith of the disciples was about to be tried. In this extended discourse, he tried to prepare them for the shock. In the days to come we will be preparing ourselves too.

But today, let's fix in our minds the necessity of trusting when we are in the shadows. Anyone can trust in the sunshine. Anyone can trust when it's easy. Faith takes on a new dimension when all the support systems are knocked down. But let me emphasize it is precisely at this point that the reality of our faith shows.

In Psalm 23 we discover why we are able to trust in the shadows. David says, "Yea, though I walk through the valley of the shadow of death, I will fear no evil, *for thou art with me*" (v. 4, KJV). Faith is for all of life because Christ is for all of life.

124

There is never an experience that can block his presence. No obstacle can quench his power. We can trust him for all situations because he is *in* all situations.

We need to remember this before the shadows come. It is harder to get hold of it in the midst of trouble. John's Gospel tells us that resurrection follows death, light comes after darkness. We can trust even in the shadows.

God, it is so hard to stand my ground in the storm. It is easier to trust you when everything is going my way than when it is not. Teach me the deep and necessary lesson of this verse today. Teach me to hold on, so that I can know the deepest victory of faith. Amen.

THE WAY IS PERSONAL

Scripture: John 14: 5-15

Text: *Lord, we don't know where you are going, so how can we know the way? (v. 5).*

If we wish to be effective disciples, we must learn the truth of this section: the way is personal.

The disciples did not see this. Thomas wanted to know the way. Philip desired to see the Father. Their questions show that the disciples had not made the discovery. We are not told specifically why they missed it, but I suspect it was because they were still trying to squeeze Jesus into the Jewish understanding of messiahship. They were still looking for the Kingdom in the wrong places. To help both Thomas and Philip, Jesus pointed them to himself. The way is personal. They would see the Father in him.

For a long time I did not see this. I tried to find the way in certain kinds of performance. I reasoned that I was surely on the way if I were doing the right things. So in my early Christian days I did everything I knew to do. I will not say that I didn't learn or grow some, but I was missing the way. What a difference when I discovered that the way was not found in my performance, but in his person.

When I first discovered the significance of John 1:14, "The Word became flesh," my life in Christ took on a new dimension. The Word is personal. After that initial intellectual discovery, I have progressed to the experiential discovery. My whole view of discipleship has been transformed!

In our quest for meaningful discipleship, we are all looking for the way. Many never find it because they depend too much on themselves and their activity. Others fail to discover it because they measure it by worldly standards. But the way is found in the person of Christ. If we will follow him, we will be on the way. The way is personal.

Father, I have spent enough time trying to stay on the way by my own efforts or someone else's standards. Help me to see today that I am on the way when I am in Christ. Amen.

NEVER ALONE

Scripture: John 14:16-31

Text: *The Spirit of truth, to be with you forever (v. 17).*

Studies have shown that one of our leading problems is loneliness. Many of us cannot stand to be by ourselves, and so we turn on stereos, televisions, or radios in order to cover up our being alone. But these are weak substitutes. We know the truth. Or do we?

The disciples feared being alone. Jesus spent quite a bit of time telling them what we need to remember: We are never alone! Never. Not for a moment! Jesus saw to that before he ever left the earth. He had already spoken to the Father about it.

He tells us that the Holy Spirit is God's means of being with us forever. In this section Jesus mentions several important ministries of the Holy Spirit that will be an aid to us in our discipleship.

First, he says the Spirit will be the *Spirit of truth*. In a time when there is so much religious quackery being practiced and taught, it is comforting to know that through the Holy Spirit we receive the truth of God.

Second, the Spirit will be our *counselor*. Today's English Version translates this word as "helper." I like that more general rendering because it is closer to the heart of the Greek, for God gives us the Holy Spirit to be our helper in any situation. If we need advice, he can be our counselor. If we need strengthening, he can be our comforter. Whatever we need, he is our helper.

Third, he is *God at home in us*. In this section Jesus is saying that through the Spirit, God resides in us. Our spirit bears witness with his Spirit. God is not detached and far away. He is in us, involved with us!

Fourth, the Spirit is the *teacher and recaller*. First, the Spirit will be our teacher. Then, having taught us the ways of God, he will bring them to our remembrance to aid us in our living and ministry. The important thing to see is that first he teaches, then he recalls. Some people expect the Spirit to fill their minds and mouths with heavenly knowledge. But Jesus reminds us that first we must study and learn the truths. Then when we have tucked them away, the Spirit will bring them to our remembrance as needed.

Fifth, the Spirit will *mediate Christ's peace*. How easy it would have been for the disciples to be restless and fearful when Jesus left. But he promised them his peace. It is not peace without substance. Rather, it is the natural result of the ministries already mentioned. If you have the Spirit of truth, if you have the divine helper, if you have God at home in you, if you have the teacher and recaller at work in you, then you don't have anything to fret about. You will have peace.

God knew that no one likes to be alone, so he provided his Spirit to be with us forever.

Lord, it helps to remember this. If I thought I had to live the Christian life by myself, I would give up. If I thought I had to be a disciple on my own, I would never try it. Thank you for being with me now and forever. With you, I am willing to give it a try. Amen.

THE VINE AND THE BRANCHES—1

Scripture: John 15:1-5

Text: *I am the vine; you are the branches (v. 5).*

You have probably had the experience of suddenly topping a hill in your car and discovering a beautiful sight. You may have pulled off to the side of the road, gotten out of your car, and looked at the scene for a long time. The beautiful vision became locked in your mind's eye. You can still recall it even though you saw it a long time ago and far away. You still feed on it.

That is the point to which we have come in John's Gospel. We are at a place where we must pull off the road and spend some time. I believe we are at the heart of discipleship in this chapter. If all of the Bible except this chapter were burned, we could reconstruct most of what discipleship is all about. So we don't want to hurry here. We want to look until what we see is locked in us.

Jesus began to talk in word-pictures. He said the life of discipleship is like the relationship between a vine and a branch. And he summed it all up in one word—we must remain (or "abide in," v. 4, RSV). Jesus was saying that if we understand how a branch abides in a vine, we can understand what it means to abide in him. And if we understand what it means to abide in him, we have discovered the secret of discipleship. Today let us examine three elements contained in "abiding."

First, to abide in Christ means there is a living connection between us and him. Between the vine and the branch is an invisible joint where the vine grows into the branch and the branch grows into the vine. It is impossible to tell where one stops and the other begins, and life passes through this connection. So with the disciple and Christ a union of life has been made that is invisible, spiritual. It is as Paul said, "For to me, to live is Christ" (Phil. 1: 21), and "It is no longer I who live, but Christ who lives in me" (Gal. 2: 20, RSV). In Paul's discipleship he had come to the place where it was hard to tell where he stopped and Christ started, and in that relationship there was the most significant sharing of life. As we grow in discipleship, we discover that a living connection has been formed between our spirit and the Spirit of Christ.

Second, the connection is continuous. The branch does not come around occasionally and receive nourishment from the vine. Instead, the branch is plugged in to the vine moment by moment. The disciple is one who is continually related to Christ, rather than being the kind of Christian whose relationship with Christ is so occasional and haphazard that it is practically worthless. The lesson is this: vitality and continuity go together. It is so for the vine and the branch. It is so for the disciple and Christ.

Third, the vine is the source. If the branch ever breaks from the vine, it begins to die. The branch must continually acknowledge and depend upon the vine as its source. The same is true for the disciple. This is not hard to see in the early days of our faith when we are so aware of our need for Christ. But as we grow in him and learn more about him, we can begin to feel more self-sufficient. It is possible to come to the point at which we say, "Thank you, God; I can take it from here." This is catastrophy for the Christian! Once the connection is made between us and Christ, he is and must always be our source. If we lose that perspective on our faith, we are in for trouble.

Jesus has let us in on the heart of the matter. Discipleship will be the exciting relationship with Christ we hope it can be if we will remember this word-picture.

Heavenly Father, thank you that I can abide in Christ like a branch abides in a vine. Thank you that it can be that life-giving, that intimate, that meaningful. Amen.

THE VINE AND THE BRANCHES—2

Scripture: John 15: 6-8

Text: *This is to my Father's glory, that you bear much fruit, showing yourselves to be my disciple (v. 8).*

Having seen the secret of discipleship and a general overview of the vine-branch relationship as it relates to abiding in Christ, we now want to look at a specific result of abiding in Christ. Jesus says that if we abide in him, we will bear fruit, and this fruitfulness will be visible proof of our discipleship. There is much for us in this analogy.

First, fruitfulness implies that no disciple is a bench warmer. On every athletic team there are a certain number of starters and a certain number of bench warmers. But in the life of Christian discipleship there are no spectators; each disciple is involved and producing for Christ. Not to be fruitful is to forfeit one's claim on discipleship.

In this regard two things need to be said. First, most churches need this message. In every congregation I know anything about, too many members have stopped producing; there is no observable fruit. Many are never seen at all. Others are mere spectators while the pastor and a core of members do most of the work. Desperately needed in our churches is the message that there is no discipleship apart from involvement.

The other word is that we dare not stereotype our fruitfulness. Not everyone will be involved in the same way, for there are varieties of service and ministry. We need to remember this and eliminate the tendency to have everyone do it our way. Many churches have been at fault by giving the impression that members must march lockstep together. If the real fruitfulness of our discipleship is to be exhibited, we must allow variety in ministry and service.

132

Now for the second idea about fruitfulness. I believe Jesus was looking forward to the time when fruitfulness would be via the Holy Spirit. He did not specifically mention the fruit of the Spirit, as Paul did in Galatians 5:22-23, but this idea is set in the context of much about the Holy Spirit. Jesus knew that fruitful discipleship was made possible by the Holy Spirit.

It is made possible in two ways. First, the Holy Spirit equips disciples for ministry through his gifts, which are listed in Romans 12:6-8; 1 Corinthians 12:4-11; 12:28; and Ephesians 4:11. If you have not done so, examine these listings of gifts and read books that describe the gifts in more detail. I recommend Dr. Kenneth Kinghorn's *Gifts of the Spirit*. Today, however, let me stress that our fruitfulness is enhanced as we discover and use our gifts.

Then, the Holy Spirit enhances our fruitfulness through his fruit, listed in Galatians 5:22-23. Whereas the gifts relate to our ministry (our doing), the fruit relates to our character (our being). And it is in the area of fruit that real spiritual maturity is measured. Jesus said, "By their fruit you will recognize them" (Matt. 7:16). Again, we have erred in the church by measuring maturity in terms of gifts. The immaturity of some Corinthian Christians, despite the presence of gifts in their lives, should show the error in doing that. It is the fruit of the Spirit that enriches our character and more perfectly conforms us to the image of Christ.

So Jesus is describing the resulting quality of vital discipleship: fruitfulness. We need to ask ourselves, "Am I becoming more and more fruitful in his service?" We can be when the Holy Spirit fills and controls us. We can know that he will enrich our character and our ministry. He takes care of the inside and the outside, and that is total!

Heavenly Father, thank you that through your Spirit you have made possible my fruitfulness. I need my attitudes enriched by your fruit. I need my actions controlled by your gifts. Come, Holy Spirit, upon me now. Amen.

THE VINE AND THE BRANCHES—3

Scripture: John 15: 9-17

Text: *Love each other as I have loved you (v. 12).*

Jesus next told his disciples to "remain" in his love (v. 9) so that they would grow in discipleship and in relationship with God the Father. But we see that this kind of abiding is accomplished through an activity: obedience. We remain in the love of Christ as we obey the commandments of God.

Here is another word that goes against the grain of some contemporary thinking. In certain quarters of the church, faith is feeling-centered and experience-oriented. Some would say, for instance, "I love you because I feel like it." So we have little pockets of believers who "love one another" because they have so much in common and because they enjoy being together so much. The problem is that some of these spiritual admiration societies have developed attitudes of intolerance and separatism from those they don't feel like loving.

The warning is clear. There is no room for this kind of immature expression of faith in discipleship. True, light cannot fellowship with darkness. But light can fellowship with light, even if the light is different. In a prism, red and green light do not have trouble fellowshiping, even though their colors are different.

Love is an act, not just an attitude. It is possible to love those who are different from you. It is possible to love those whom you may not feel like loving. Sure, it is tough. It's much harder to love like that than it is to gather around you eight or ten people who make you feel warm all over. But Jesus said obedient, unconditional love will make discipleship effective. That is love based on the will and lived in obedience to God's commands.

The beauty of this passage is that Jesus was not vague. If he had stopped after saying, "Love one another," we could have classified him with all other moralists. But he fleshed out his words by adding, "as I have loved you." We do not have to wonder what he meant; he showed us with his life. He loved us despite our differences. He loved us sacrificially. He loved us by giving up his life for us.

Jesus talked about "fruit that will last" (v. 16). The only kind of fruit in our discipleship that will last is fruitfulness based on obedient love, willful love, sacrificial love, life-giving love. "The fruit of the Spirit is love" (Gal. 5:22).

Lord, I need a baptism of love. Not just the mushy-gushy kind, but the tough kind that keeps on going in obedience when feelings have fallen by the wayside. That's the only kind of love that will bring us together as Christians, the only kind that will make an impression on the world. Even pagans love those who love them. Give me your real love, Lord Jesus. Amen.

THE VINE AND THE BRANCHES—4

Scripture: John 15:18—16:4

Text: *If the world hates you, keep in mind that it hated me first (15:18).*

The final picture in the vine-branch relationship is one of logical consequence. Jesus told his disciples plainly that they can expect to receive from the world what he received because they will be reflecting his ministry.

This idea coincides with the vine-branch picture. If you put poison at the root system of a tree, it will rise through the trunk and eventually work its way out to the branches. In the same way, if the world expresses hatred of Christ, in time this hatred would work its way into the disciples' ministry. They were to expect this and make their commitment to discipleship with this in mind.

So should we. It is hard to realize that authentic discipleship is not without its cost and persecution. This is especially hard to realize in America, where we profess our faith in safety and comfort. But these words of Jesus should bring us back to reality and to the strengthening of our commitment. Many believers in the world already know the reality of our text. In other countries, doors seem to be closing to the spread of the gospel. One church analyst has said there would be more persecution of Christians in the twentieth century than in the previous nineteen combined. We dare not get so complacent as to believe it can't happen here. We dare not build a faith and a commitment that omit this truth.

Yet, while widespread persecution is missing in America, persecution still exists. I have met Christians who were shunned by family members. I have known Christians who were ridiculed because of certain ethical and moral stands they took in their vocations. I have counseled some young people who said, "Mom and Dad are not going to like it when they find out I've become a Christian."

Jesus has told us in advance that as it is for the vine so shall it be for the branch. Only with this perspective can we remain truly entwined with the vine who is our life. Only with this understanding of discipleship can we understand that even for the Christian there are fair winds and foul.

God, give me a faith that can take it. I do thank you that I live in a nation in which religious freedom is granted. But I know there are still battles to be fought and storms to be weathered. I want to stand for Christ regardless of the situation. By your grace, grant me this ability. Amen.

BETTER THAT HE'S GONE?

Scripture: John 16:5-11

Text: *It is for your good that I am going away (v. 7).*

If I could have one wish, it would be to spend fifteen minutes talking face to face with Jesus. There is much I would like to ask him. Other Christians have said, "Wouldn't it be great if Jesus could be here in person," so this attitude is not uncommon.

But Jesus told his disciples, with whom he had spoken face to face, that it was better for them that he go away. That must have sounded strange, for how could anything be better than actually being with Jesus? Why is it better for you and me that Jesus is not actually with us in a physical body?

For one thing, it is better because now he can be *in* us, not just *with* us. As long as Christ was in his physical body, he could not enter into another's life, but now he can. Paul said the real secret of the gospel was "Christ in you, the hope of glory" (Col. 1:27). *Christ in you!* There is no way that could happen while he was on earth. But now that he has gone and come again in the Spirit, he can actually reside in us. Our bodies become his temple; he lives in us. And that's better.

It is also better because now he is not limited by space and time. As long as Christ was physically on earth, he could only be in one place. If he were here today, he could only be in one place. Suppose he were in your town today. That would be great for you, but what about other Christians? There's no way he could get around to all of us. But now that he has gone away and come again in the Spirit, he can be with me as I write these words and with you as you read them. Time cannot hold him; he is not limited to a particular place. And that's better.

Third, it is better because now he doesn't just do things *for* us; he does things *to* and *through* us. Don't misunderstand. There is never a time when Christ does not do things for us, whether physically present or absent, for he is always our source. But as long as he was in a physical body, there was a sense of dependence that limited the disciples' ministry and their effectiveness. Now that he is with us and in us through the Spirit, he works with us in a new way. We become the vessels through which he fulfills his ministry in the world. To be sure, this defies description. It is the difference between standing and observing a power plant producing electricity, and actually having the power plant in you, producing electricity. And that's better.

I would still like to be able to spend fifteen minutes face to face with Jesus. That desire will never go away, but it's not the best. The best is the way it is now. Christ left the world physically so he could return spiritually. Now he dwells within me and all believers everywhere. He is creatively working out his ministry through us. And that's better.

Lord, I am growing in my understanding of what you told your disciples. Yes, I would like to visit with you face to face, but deep down I know that it is better the way it is. Thank you for making it better. Amen.

HE SPEAKS TODAY

Scripture: John 16:12-15

Text: *I have much more to say to you (v. 12).*

It is fantastic to know Jesus' teaching ministry did not stop with his physical presence. In this teaching section of John's Gospel, Jesus indicated that he had even more to teach the disciples, and he related that future teaching ministry to the coming of the Holy Spirit. Luke records in the Book of Acts that the Gospels were merely the records of what Jesus *began* to do and to teach. The Book of Acts is our first glimpse into Jesus' continuing ministry through the Spirit.

We believe Jesus speaks today. We believe his ministry is still living and active and that he continues to teach and guide his disciples.

First, Jesus speaks today through Scripture. No Christian believes that the Bible is only a record of past events. We claim with the author of Hebrews that God's Word is living today, as it was then. We believe Christ communicates today through both the Old and New Testaments. The Spirit first inspired the writers, and now he enables us to interpret Scripture.

On several occasions I have been with authors and discussed their works. I always have received additional insight into their writings, for there simply is nothing like talking with the authors themselves.

The same is true as we read the Bible. Since the Spirit who was present with those who wrote the Bible is here with us, what a joyous time we can have communing with him as we study the Word.

Second, Jesus speaks today through the Spirit's direct ministry. Jesus said, "He will bring glory to me by taking from what is mine and making it known to you" (v. 14). We must remember that the Holy Spirit's ministry is always to glorify Christ, never himself, by taking what is Christ's—what he hears from Christ—and communicating it to disciples.

We also must remember that the Spirit's words will never contradict what God says in Scripture. Today's disciple should not fear a new word from God, but he must always check it against the sufficient revelation in Scripture. He must shy away from any private or exclusive revelations, and test the spirits to see if they are from God.

Having run the tests, we disciples must be constantly open to the voice of Christ leading and guiding. The Spirit speaks directly to our spirit through such things as suggestions, inclinations, motivations, and thoughts. Less frequently, the Spirit uses dreams. He also speaks to us through other believers, whose counsel, advice, and exhortation must be taken seriously. And he speaks through world situations, for as we are gripped by the world and its needs, Jesus speaks to us about our ministry, stewardship, and service.

I am glad Christ did not stop speaking when his physical ministry ended. I am glad he still has a word for me—a word through Scripture, through the Spirit, through believers, through inner impressions, through a needy world.

Listen. What is he saying to you?

Speak, Lord, thy servant heareth. Amen.

IN JESUS' NAME

Scripture: John 16:16-30

Text: *My Father will give you whatever you ask in my name (v. 23).*

While I was conducting a prayer seminar in a west Texas town, a lady asked, "What does it mean to pray 'in Jesus' name'?" Since then I have been asked that question on several occasions. It seems to be a sincere question from people interested in discipleship. Jesus relates a vital prayer life to praying "in his name," so we need to understand this phrase.

First, to pray in Jesus' name is to pray with a spirit and desire like his. What is that desire? "Not my will, but thine, be done" (Luke 22:42, KJV). To pray in Jesus' name is to pray desiring God's will to be done in whatever we pray for.

This seems obvious, but it takes a while to reach this point in discipleship and prayer. Most of us continue to struggle with it throughout our Christian experience. Despite my intellectual desire for God's will to prevail, I often pray from other desires and motives. God knows this. He does not punish me for my mixed motives or my misguided petitions, but he helps me see that prayer is much stronger and more on target when my highest desire is for his will to be done.

Second, to pray in Jesus' name is to pray realizing where the resources are. As I pray for this or that, I am realizing that ultimately the answers come from Christ, who is "able to do far more abundantly than all that we ask or think" (Eph. 3:20, RSV). As a Christian, I have the privilege of drawing on the resources of Christ. A teacher on prayer said, It's like going to the bank to withdraw a million dollars. The bank would not honor such a request if I tried to get the money on the strength of my name. But if I had the authorization from a multimillionaire friend, they would let me have the money. In prayer we may ask for the resources of heaven, because as brothers in Christ we are authorized to approach the Father in his name.

Third, to pray in Jesus' name speaks of the quality of my relationship. Notice that Jesus did not say to pray *with* his name, but *in* it. The early church had some trouble with this when certain people tried to use the name of Jesus like a magical incantation. But it didn't work; the name of Jesus is not magic. We don't tack these words on at the end of a prayer to validate everything else we have said. Rather, they are symbolic of an existing relationship. We are *in* Christ. Christ is *in* us. Hence, we can pray *in* his name.

The prayer of the disciple will be "in Jesus' name." It will be a prayer that is prayed from a desire for God's will to be done, a prayer that dares to draw on the resources of heaven, a prayer that is prayed out of a vital relationship with the master. That kind of prayer, Jesus said, will get results.

Father, I confess that too much of my praying is too vague. I know that the words "in Jesus' name" tacked on at the end of my prayer are not what really matters. What does matter is what those words mean. Help me to pray in the spirit of those words. Amen.

THE OVERCOMERS

Scripture: John 16:31-33

Text: *Take heart! I have overcome the world (v. 33).*

Jesus concluded his extended teaching to the disciples on a note of triumph with an astounding claim. He has overcome the world, the whole world, and everything in the world! This was a message the disciples would need to remember during the fearful hours that lay ahead. Jesus said that because he has overcome the world, they can take heart. In what sense did he overcome the world? In two ways, each of which can cause us to take heart today.

First, Jesus overcame the world at that moment in his spirit. Very soon he would be taken into custody and be a prisoner. He would be under heavy guard. He would suffer. He would die. He knew all that, but he still was an overcomer. His spirit was free! No chains could hold him.

A prisoner in a concentration camp was beaten within an inch of his life, but he still refused to talk. Finally, in desperation, one of the camp's commanders said, "We might as well kill him." A guard who had been with the prisoner most of the time spoke up, "You may take his life, but you cannot kill him." That's the way it was with Christ. They beat him, mocked him, and crucified him, but they could not kill him! He was free. He had overcome the world.

We can take heart in this because we can know the same kind of spiritual victory in life. Two recent experiences in my pastorate have confirmed this. The first was a lady's long struggle with cancer. Together with her family, she and I walked through some dark valleys. Finally we had to walk through the valley of death itself. Disease did its worst, but it did not kill her! Many days before the final crisis, she won the victory in her spirit. She was free. The other experience is still in process. In a few days, another lady I know is going to a large medical center for surgery for a rare disease. There is every chance she may die. We have talked, prayed, and taken Holy Communion together. Prepared for the worst, this woman is ready. She is free. She has overcome the world—*now!* We can take heart that when the world hurls the worst it can at us, we can still be overcomers in our spirits.

The second victory for Christ was his sure knowledge that what was about to happen to him would set the stage for the coming of the Kingdom. This element of overcoming would not happen immediately. Nonetheless, as Christ looked down the corridors of time, he saw it. He had overcome the world in the ultimate sense. One day the kingdoms of this world will be replaced by the Kingdom of God and his Christ. He saw it!

At times I wonder about the future of the faith. At times I wonder about the future of the church. Sometimes the available evidence does not look good. But then, I lift up my eyes and see that the final victory is Christ's! What he did nearly two thousand years ago has broken Satan's back once and for all. There are still some clean-up campaigns, but the war is over! We can sing with the hymn writer, "I know not what the future holds, but I know who holds the future."

Take heart today as a disciple. Christ has overcome the world. He has overcome it in his spirit, and he shows us we can do the same. He has overcome it for the ages, and he promises us that we shall share in that victory.

Father, when I am prone to wonder or even to despair, let me remember these words of Jesus, the overcomer. Let them make me an overcomer too! Amen.

THE GREAT PRAYER—1

Scripture: John 17:1-5

Text: *Father, the time has come. Glorify your Son (v. 1).*

While we call the words we repeat in church "the Lord's Prayer," this prayer of Jesus, called by the scholars "the high-priestly prayer," is really his prayer. In it are the climax and fulfillment of our Lord's earthly ministry. Often Jesus had said his "time had not yet come" (7:30). But now he says, "The time has come." Everything toward which he had been moving since that first night in Bethlehem was at hand. The reason the Word had become flesh was there. He had given them the symbols of the New Covenant in the Last Supper. He had given the example of service through washing their feet. He had instructed them in the things that make for vitality and victory. The time had come to secure it all through the giving of his life. And being true to his nature, Jesus prayed.

In this prayer he prayed for three things: himself, the immediate group of disciples, and all believers. In the next several days we will examine each of these dimensions, but today we will look at how Jesus prayed for himself. He says that through the coming experiences his supreme desire is that God will glorify him. Where is the glory in what is about to happen to Christ?

First, there is glory in that his death on the cross will be the means of eternal life for many. His authority, which extended to so many areas during his earthly ministry, now encompasses the final area—the destiny of men. There is glory in that he can give eternal life to those who seek it through him.

Second, there is glory because his ministry is perfected. Tear out the remaining pages of the Gospel at this point and Jesus becomes one of many great men. But put in the hours of ordeal and the hours of the cross, and the purpose for his coming is completed. Glorification is possible because he has left nothing undone. From the cross he cried, "It is finished" (19:30). All has been done.

Third, there is glory because he has honored the Father through perfect obedience. In leaving nothing undone, Christ has fulfilled the eternal plan of God. In return, Christ will receive the glory he had before the world began. He will ascend and put on the robes of glory. Glory begun on earth will be consummated in heaven.

Lest we think that Christ is praying here that he will "stand out," we need to remember the real meaning of *glory*. It is not that someone is in the spotlight. In Scripture, *glory* usually means that the excellence of something is made known. When Christ prayed for his glorification, he prayed that the full significance of his ministry might be made known. He prayed that his ministry might reach its full potential of excellence. Such was the nature of his glory, and we have beheld it!

Dear God, thank you that you glorified Christ. Thank you that the purpose and excellence of his ministry were made known through the hours that followed, and that two-thousand years later people are still seeing the excellence of it. Amen.

THE GREAT PRAYER—2

Scripture: John 17:6-19

Text: *I pray for them . . . for those you have given me (v. 9).*

Jesus' love for his disciples is clearly seen in this part of the prayer. I am convinced Jesus hated to leave this band of men who had become his family. He had invested everything in them. On the night of his betrayal, he prayed for them that they might be able to carry on the work he had called them to do.

Jesus prayed mainly for their protection, a recurring theme throughout this section. He knew it was going to get rough. These men would have it harder than any of them imagined because Satan would unleash all his fury on them and the world would attack them. In the end, many of them would die martyrs' deaths. So Jesus prayed for God's protection for them and for specific results of that protection.

First, there would be unity. If God did not protect them, they would be scattered like sheep. But with his protection they would remain unified, as Christ intended them to be. We shall see later how close they came to being scattered and losing their purpose.

Second, there would be joy, not just any joy, but the joy of Christ within them. Left to themselves, they would despair. But with God's protection, they would have joy in knowing they were continuing Christ's ministry in the world and that God within them was greater than Satan, their attacker.

Third, there would be sanctification. This word is not heard often in church circles anymore, but it is an important biblical term that Jesus used for a significant purpose. Basically it has two meanings: to set apart for sacred use, and to cleanse and make holy. These men had been designated "apostles" (Luke 6:13) and sent into the world to perpetuate the gospel and extend the Kingdom. Everything depended on them. They were set apart; they were special. They needed God's protection to remain set apart, but they also needed it to live holy lives. Christ prayed for their inward and outward sanctification for their character and their ministry.

How was this protection to come? I believe it was through the Holy Spirit about whom Jesus has told them. Through the Spirit the disciples would find their unity, and through him they would rejoice. By the Spirit they would be set apart and cleansed.

Remember that this section of the prayer was specifically for the apostles; that is the context. But we can assume that Christ wills the same protection for us today. The gospel still opposes Satan's purposes. We still need the Spirit's protection or we will lose our unity and strength. Without God's protection we cannot have joy or remain set apart in our service or cleansed in our lives.

Heavenly Father, let the protective presence of your Holy Spirit surround me and infill me today. Amen.

THE GREAT PRAYER—3

Scripture: John 17: 20-26

Text: *I pray also for those who will believe in me through their message (v. 20).*

Did you know Christ prayed for you before he left this world? That prayer is recorded in this section. Looking down the corridors of time, Jesus prayed for every person who would come to faith through the witness of the apostles, including you and me.

Each of us has a spiritual family tree. If you were to tell me who was most instrumental in leading you to Christ, we could then go to that person and ask him or her the same question. If we continued this process far enough, we would arrive back at the feet of one of these apostles; so it is through their message that we are here today. The important thing to see is what he prayed for. What did he want to happen to you and me as future believers?

First, Jesus prayed that we might be one. He prayed for our unity even as he prayed for the unity of the first apostles. Unity is his desire for every generation of believers, because "united we stand; divided we fall." Jesus knew that division among believers weakens our attack on evil and destroys our witness to society.

Did Jesus intend for our unity to be expressed through one superchurch? Some church leaders think so. I do not agree. I do not believe it is denominationalism per se that is weakening us. Denominations by and large exist to minister to people of different personality types. Some prefer worship to be more formal; others like it free. In a sense, I see denominations as one of the ways God uses to minister to people who are not alike. I believe Jesus was praying for a unity that transcends denominations. We can have our various denominations and approaches as long as we remember that the church is made up of all who profess Christ. And I believe we are seeing this prayer answered in our time, when there is less and less concern for denominationalism. God is renewing believers in all denominations and creating a unity of spirit, not structure. This kind of unity binds us together with invisible cords, and within it the total body of Christ finds new strength and life.

Second, Jesus prayed that the world might believe through our message. The church exists in the world to bring others into the fellowship of faith. Evangelism has often been viewed with suspicion and disinterest, but it is regaining importance and integrity in several major denominations. We should praise God for this, and pray that the emerging forms of evangelism will be true to his Word. Since many in the world are hungry for the quality of life that Christ offers, we may be on the verge of a great revival if our evangelism is true to the gospel.

Third, Jesus prayed that we might join him in heaven. After I shared this truth with one group, a man said in amazement, "Never before have I realized that Jesus actually prayed for me to go to heaven." Christ wants you to go; he has already prayed to the Father about it.

Fourth, Jesus prayed that we might be aware of his love and presence. When statesman Daniel Webster was asked to share his greatest thought, he replied, "The greatest thought I have ever had is this, God loves me." Jesus knew that to be aware of the love of God is to be transformed, so he prayed for this in us. But that awareness is not of a loving God who is far away. We know God loves us because he lives in us!

As growing disciples, we need to study this section of the prayer carefully and return to it often. It will continue to nourish and strengthen us. Christ has prayed for our unity with other believers, our witness to the world, our eternal destiny, and our awareness of his love and presence.

Thank you, Lord, for praying for me. Thank you that right at this moment you are at the right hand of the Father interceding for me. This assurance helps me live as a disciple. Amen.

THE MAJESTY AND THE MAN

Scripture: John 18:1-9

Text: *I am he (v. 5).*

John does not describe the prayer period in the garden. Instead, he focuses on the act of betrayal and shows us the majesty of Christ in this section.

We begin with a curious situation. Judas was leading the soldiers to the place where Jesus was, and John says that a whole detachment of soldiers went to make the arrest. In his commentary, William Barclay explains the Greek word translated "detachment," pointing out that it can have three meanings. If we take the largest number it can represent, it stands for 1,000 men—240 cavalry, and 760 infantrymen. And if we take the smallest number it is used to describe, 200 men are still in the force. Amazing, isn't it, that such an army would be sent out to bring back one man? That is quite a compliment to the power of Jesus.

But notice what happens. When this whole array of soldiers arrives and asked for Jesus, he said, "I am he." Three simple, quiet words. And the army fell to the ground! Scholars have speculated that one soldier stumbled and had a domino effect on the rest. I don't know. But I do know that something happened to the group. They were amazed.

People were always amazed at the presence of Jesus. The crowds listened to his teachings and were gripped by his unique authority, and they said, "No one ever spoke the way this man does" (7:46). Simon Peter first encountered his majesty and cried, "Depart from me; for I am a sinful man, O Lord" (Luke 5:8, KJV). The woman at the well was awestruck to meet a man who knew her like he did. The woman caught in adultery would never forget being thrown at his feet. The multitude would forever remember the sight of his triumphal entry.

Peter Marshall describes a striking encounter with Christ in his sermon "Gallery Christians." Jo Betts, a seafood distributor, met Christ one day at his work. Marshall says, "Later that morning, when business was in full swing, Jo suddenly looked up to see a strange man standing in the doorway. He wore a quite ordinary-looking, blue-serge business suit. But somehow there was nothing ordinary about the man. It was his eyes Jo noticed especially. The fish merchant was no poet, but there was something luminous . . . yes that was it, luminous—and compelling about them."

The majesty and the man go together. Meditate on that today. He comes to us as one who overwhelms us, but he does not overpower us in any brutish way. Three words—"I am he"—derail an army. But then, three words he spoke captured my life and yours—"I want you."

Lord Jesus, your quiet majesty is overwhelming. You are my king. Amen.

SWORDS AND SALVATION

Scripture: John 18:10-11

Text: *Put your sword away! (v. 11).*

From this point on in the Gospel, we see a very stormy period for Simon Peter. Everything fell apart. He had so much trouble getting it back together. Even when he promised to do right, he did wrong. You can hear the threads tearing out the seams of his life.

It began in the garden. In the middle of the encounter, Peter pulled his sword. A suicidal act! We've already noted the size of the detachment of soldiers. What on earth did Peter think he was doing? Surely he didn't think he could defend Jesus against that mob. No. Peter wasn't thinking at all. He had hit the panic button.

Jesus spoke up for the first time, sternly. "Put your sword away!" I think Jesus meant, "Peter, swords and salvation do not go together. The Kingdom will not come by trying to fight it out with your enemies. If you fall prey to that kind of thinking, you have lost your perspective on discipleship and the Kingdom."

Jesus had just finished telling the disciples to expect opposition, hatred, and persecution. He also had told them that in such times they could know God's protection. Knowing this, the tactics for disciples would be different from the tactics of the world.

There is still a message here for us. There have been times when we have drawn swords against those who oppose us. We have attacked, criticized, and withdrawn from those who did not see it our way. By our attitudes and actions we have often weakened the effect of the gospel rather than enhanced it. Salvation is wholeness, and we don't bring wholeness to people by chopping them up or cutting them down.

A story from my childhood illustrates this point. One afternoon my friend and I were playing hockey in my front yard when my friend's sister came over and for some reason said to me, "You're not a Christian."

Well, I thought I was as much a Christian as I could be at my age, and I knew I was as much a Christian as she was. So I said, "Oh, yes, I am a Christian!"

She said, "No, you're not."

It happened that my friend and I had roller skates on. So I proceeded to kick the girl into a chain-link fence, all the time saying, "I am too a Christian! I am too a Christian!" Even as a child I learned some things from that experience.

And I've learned more in the same area since. We don't prove our spirituality by exposing someone else's lack of it. If we try that approach we will soon have all our dirty laundry on the line right along with theirs. As a disciple, I am learning that I must not "repay anyone evil for evil" (Rom. 12:17). If I do, I wind up no better than those I oppose.

And I am learning that I don't have to defend Jesus. He can take care of himself; he has been doing so for nearly two-thousand years. My little drawn sword is not going to make that much difference. I'll only end up hurting others and getting hurt myself.

What I am learning is that people are won by love, patience, and kindness. This does not mean that we compromise the gospel. It means that we live it. I cannot anticipate or control another's actions, but I can control my reactions.

John doesn't tell us that Jesus healed the man's ear, but Luke does. Jesus healed one of his enemies. In the life of discipleship we need to be more concerned with mending relationships than breaking them. That's the Kingdom way.

Lord, I admit I have a sword and at times I get pleasure in using it. Help me to see this is not the Kingdom way. Amen.

SOMETHING CROWS WHEN IT HAPPENS

Scripture: John 18:12-18, 25-27

Text: *Again Peter denied it, and at that moment a rooster began to crow (v. 27).*

Here was the all-time low for Peter. Gripped with fear, Peter began to say and do things he thought he would never do. Later, as he reflected upon it, I am sure he could hardly believe it happened. But it did.

We don't want to be too hard on Peter. Each of us has known moments of denial or compromise. We too have asked ourselves, "How could I have done (or said, or thought) that?" But we did. What I would like for you to see today is that something "crows" in us when we do it. If we are truly disciples, we cannot deny or compromise our faith without something happening to us.

I know a Christian man who heard the call of God to enter the ordained ministry. But he tried to compromise that call, averting it for years. Now, thank God, he has responded and found his place in life. But he says he felt a real misery deep in his soul during the days of evasion. Something was crowing in him.

I know another man who at this very moment has compromised the ethics and morality of his faith. In hoping to get away with it, he is having to deny and rationalize his actions. Something is crowing in him. Maybe he will hear it.

I know still another man who several years ago fell prey to alcohol addiction. Ashamed of his problem, he dropped out of active church life and went all the way to the bottom. But something was crowing in him. He heard it! And today he is doing all he can to find healing.

We simply cannot compromise our faith and get by with it.

There are plenty of opportunities to do so. There were for Peter; there are for us. But we dare not. I know a pastor who had the opportunity to take a little money from church funds. He thought no one would ever know, and they didn't. But getting by with it only fed a neurotic desire to keep doing it. I choose to believe something crowed in this man, but he turned a deaf ear to it and went on in his dishonesty. But it didn't last. He was caught. Today he is out of the ministry, living away from God.

The warning is clear. Don't deny Christ. I would rather be called a fanatic than a fool.

Lord, I know that I have not always been true to my convictions. I, too, am a sinner, fallen short of your glory. But in my heart I know what I want to do. Help me to do it. Thank you that something crowed in Peter's life and brought him to his senses. Use whatever you have to in order to bring me to my senses and keep me there. Amen.

BLINDERS

Scripture: John 18:19-24

Text: *If I spoke the truth, why did you hit me? (v. 23).*

"Don't confuse me with the facts; my mind is made up."

This was the motto of the Jews who sought to kill Jesus. They questioned Jesus, but it was mere formality. They knew what they were going to do, and they spared nothing to get the job done. Facing the Holy One of God, they still chose their prejudices over his power. This is one of the ironies of human nature. It is as if we are wearing blinders. We just can't seem to see, or we don't want to. It can work either way.

During my seminary days I was assigned to work for eight weeks in a storefront mission in downtown Lexington, Kentucky. On weekends I would go there with others to attempt to minister to drunks living in that part of town. One whom I will never forget was Charles. There was something different about him, and He liked me. For several weeks we really hit it off. I thought things were progressing. Then one weekend I went to the mission and Charles wasn't there. Some of the other men told me he was in a bar around the corner, so I left to find him. And I did.

He was seated in a booth with a friend and two female companions. As I walked over to where he was, a tipsy barmaid stumbled and spilled a bottle of beer down my pants and into my shoes. Charles jumped up and tried to dry me off. Because he was interested in me, I thought maybe I could get through to him spiritually. I asked him to walk outside with me. For the next two hours we talked. Charles finally said, "It's no use. It's just not for me. There's nothing left for me but to go to hell." Nothing I could say made any difference. He had blinders on. I am sure there are other Charleses in the world—people who just can't seem to see the grace of God and the truth of Christ.

But even more tragic than these are the people who are aware of the differences and who know the alternatives. Right now I know a man who, I am convinced, has decided he would rather have his sin than his Savior. He is to be pitied, because he made the choice to leave the blinders alone.

This is what the Jews did. They could have acknowledged Christ. Sure, they would have had to confess that they had been wrong about Jesus. They would have had to do some backtracking. They could have been embarrassed. But it would have been worth it all!

In the life of discipleship we must guard against prejudging. We must guard against refusing to change our minds even in the face of the evidence. Pride *does* go before a fall, and some falls are hard to recover from.

Dear Lord, give me eyes that really see. Make my vision clear, not obscured. Also give me grace to admit when I am wrong, and the willingness to work to make things right. Let me swallow my pride lest I get swallowed by it. Amen.

THE WAY OF EXPEDIENCY

Scripture: John 18:28—19:16

Text: *I find no basis for a charge against him (19:6).*

Pilate is one of the tragic characters of Scripture. In studying and restudying this story, I am increasingly convinced that he was a just man trying to do what was right.

For one thing, Pilate investigated Jesus intently and fairly, not like the kangaroo court of the Jews. Pilate questioned Jesus sincerely and concluded that there was no basis for the charge leveled against him.

Pilate also gave indication of being a searching man. It appears that he was somewhat interested in Jesus' description of the Kingdom. And he asked the question that still haunts many, "What is truth?" (18:38). We do not know if Pilate ever found out the answer to that question. But we do know that he commanded a sign to be placed on the cross, "Jesus of Nazareth, the King of the Jews" (19:19). When the enraged Jews tried to get him to change it, Pilate answered, "What I have written, I have written" (19:22). The Galilean had made some impact on this Roman governor.

So there are some things that are commendable in Pilate. But his problem was that he tried to be all things to all men. He didn't want to offend anyone. He wanted to do the expedient thing. And it backfired. I am convinced that when Pilate gave the people a choice of whom to release, he fully expected them to call for the release of Jesus. The contrast was too obvious. Barabbas was a known criminal who had led a rebellion. Jesus was the one who had brought the healing love of God to many in the city. He was the one Pilate could find no fault in. When Pilate heard the crowd scream for the release of Barabbas and the crucifixion of Jesus, I believe he was shocked to his soul. But it was too late. His attempt to be expedient had turned on him. He had set the conditions; now he had to live by them. He had to live with them for the rest of his life.

If Peter's denial tells us of the peril of compromise, Pilot's example warns us against trying to be in the good graces of everyone. It simply cannot be done. To take a stand is to assure opposition from someone; to take no stand is to forfeit discipleship. Not to stand is really a vote against Christ. Even Jesus said, "You are neither cold nor hot. I wish you were either one or the other! So because you are lukewarm . . . I am about to spit you out of my mouth" (Rev. 3:15-16).

There was a time in my life when I tried to calculate what people would think of me. Consequently, I often softened my position to keep from risking their displeasure. Thanks to the keen observation of my wife and the prodding of the Spirit, I have given up that way of life. Today I will take my stand for Christ as clearly as I can and as close to his will as I can. This is the way of discipleship.

Father, help me to take a stand for Christ. I do not wish to be offensive or obnoxious or unloving. But I do wish to be known as a person who lives by his convictions and for Christ. Save me from the trap of expediency. Amen.

HYPOCRISY!

Scripture: John 19:1-6

Text: *We have no king but Caesar (v. 15).*

The chief priest here reveals the sordid end of man's spirit. The rulers were trying Jesus on grounds of blasphemy, but they were guilty of blasphemy in claiming allegiance to Caesar rather than to God. Judas was paid thirty pieces of silver for Jesus. These men sold out for nothing.

One of my seminary professors said, "Hypocrisy is the sin of the saints." He went on to say that outright sinners are not guilty of hypocrisy. They care nothing for Christ and they let you know it. That's not hypocrisy—that's honesty.

It's the people who claim to be closest to God who fall prey to this sin, and the chief priests would have claimed to be closest of all. They professed a faith in God as their sovereign, but they were willing to switch their allegiance. Once Jesus was on the cross, then they could return to their high-sounding theology about God their king.

John seems to be going out of his way to show the possibility of selling out. First Peter. Then Pilate. Now the priests. Who next? Not us, we hope. Perhaps John is warning us that hypocrisy is still the sin of the saints.

The words "we have no king but Caesar" rise up to haunt these Jews when Titus destroyed Jerusalem in *A.D.* 70. When we speak with forked tongues, we will be found out too. One night during my college days, I went into a restaurant where several of my college buddies were. As we were sitting there, one of my friends who was pastoring a little church in the country said, "Well, I wonder what fairy tale I'm going to tell my people this week." I was stunned. I was speechless. I could not believe he had said it. Hypocrisy! And it got him. Today he is nowhere to be found in the ordained ministry, and I do not know if he is even professing Christ.

We have seen fear, expediency, and unjust goals cause men's downfalls. Watch out! "The devil prowls around like a roaring lion, seeking some one to devour" (I Pet. 5:8, RSV). He is not trying to devour the sinners; he already has them. He's looking for some would-be saint who is vulnerable. Don't be a statistic.

God, I confess that as a disciple I am a candidate for the attacks of Satan. I know that only by your grace can I withstand. I seek this grace today with my whole heart. Let my eye be single and my purpose clear. Amen.

GOD'S NEW FAMILY

Scripture: John 19:16-27

Text: *Here is your son . . . Here is your mother (vv. 26, 27).*

Jesus created a new family. This is seen from the passage just read, and it is highlighted even more clearly in Mark 3:34-35 when Jesus said, "Here are my mother and my brothers! Whoever does God's will is my brother and sister and mother." The new family is based on spiritual ties, not physical. A person's physical brothers and sisters may or may not be his spiritual brothers and sisters. People with whom we have no earthly kinship may be dear brothers and sisters to us. The church is to be the family of God, bringing this deep relationship of caring and fellowship to those who make it up. In our discipleship we need to be concerned about cultivating relationships in this new family.

There are places in the world where this stands out more graphically than in America. When I was in India, we spent a week in Madras, where we worshiped at the Emmanuel Methodist Church with Dr. Sam Kamalesan and his congregation. At the conclusion of the worship service, it was announced that there would be a baptismal service. The crowd of over five hundred filed into the church's courtyard where the baptistry was. There we sang, prayed, and witnessed the baptism of a girl in her late teens or early twenties. She had been converted from a Muslim background. Later we learned that when she professed faith in Christ, her family ostracized her. When she left home that morning for church, she was told that if she was baptized as a Christian there was no need to come home. Think of the agony of her decision! But rejoice in the fact that Christians in the fellowship took her into their family. She would now be their daughter. I saw the new family in operation that day.

While we may never face that kind of decision or make such

a drastic break with those we love, we should ever be mindful that we are members of God's new family. I am convinced that the churches that discover this quality of community and fellowship will be the churches that are most alive. Our discipleship will certainly be more vital when we realize that the church is not a conglomerate of unrelated individuals but a family of people related to each other in a very important way.

In physical families we like to claim kinship on the basis of bloodlines. Today I want you to see that you are related to every believer. We have the blood of Christ as our unity!

Father, thank you for giving me more brothers and sisters than I could ever imagine. I praise and thank you for my physical family relations. But I thank you that there is a deeper spiritual relationship in your new family and that many with whom I have no physical ties are my dear spiritual relatives. Thank you that some of my physical relatives are also spiritual relatives, which makes it even better. Thank you for making me a part of so rich a spiritual family. Amen.

DONE!

Scripture: John 19:28-37

Text: *It is finished* (v. 30).

These are the three greatest words ever spoken. They are not words of defeat or depression but words of victory. The Greek word *tetelestai*, derived from the root form *telos*, means to consummate, fully perform, or bring to a perfect end. Implied are the ideas of fulfillment, realization, and thoroughness. Such was the nature of the cry Jesus gave.

In these words Jesus was highlighting his fulfillment of the plan of God since the foundation of the world. John the Baptist had exclaimed, "Behold, the Lamb of God, who takes away the sin of the world!" (1:29, RSV). That exclamation linked Jesus with the Old Testament's rich imagery of the sacrificial, atoning Lamb. It took the hearers back to the very first Passover in Egypt and declared that Jesus would now be God's eternal Passover. All of the Old Testament prototypes of salvation found their climax in this exclamation of Jesus.

The significance of this is well known to most Christians. In evangelical circles the preaching of the cross is central. Yet we can get accustomed to hearing it. We can fail to be gripped by it. Today, remember the eternal significance of Christ's death on the cross. The hymn writer has captured it by saying, "Yea, *all* I need in thee to find, O Lamb of God, I come."

John highlights the victory by adding, "he bowed his head" (19:30). A more literal rendering from the Greek would be "inclined." The idea is that of resting his head. All the pressure and tension were gone. The deed had been done; rest could be taken.

Today as you go about your tasks, think of the perfect work of Christ on the cross. Think of his perfect fulfillment of the plan of God. His sacrifice is the key to your life in him, the key to your discipleship. Take this away and there is nothing;

discipleship is impossible. You can rest in Christ because of his work.

Listen to the hymn writer again: "Safe in the arms of Jesus, safe on His gentle breast. There by His love o'er shaded, sweetly my soul shall rest."

Lord Jesus, thank you for going to the cross for me. Thank you for going there to finish perfectly the task for which you were sent into the world. In my spiritual life, let me never get to the place where I am not gripped and moved by what you have done. Amen.

NEVER GIVE UP

Scripture: John 19:38-42

Text: *He was accompanied by Nicodemus (v. 39).*

Suddenly Nicodemus reappears in the narrative. We have not seen him since chapter 7, and then only briefly. It has really been since chapter 3 that we have met him in any detail. There that he had the extended conversation with Jesus and first heard about the possibility and necessity of new birth. In chapter 7, Nicodemus stood before his fellow leaders to say that justice required a fair hearing for Jesus, but beyond that there is no indication of any commitment on his part.

Yet, I think it is significant that John mentions the presence of Nicodemus at this time. Evidently something had been stirring around in him. He never was able to shake that first encounter with Christ. A seed was planted, and I dare to believe it was sprouting. Nicodemus is not mentioned in Scripture again, so we are left to speculate about him. But I believe he went on to become a follower of the way. His name means "victory over the people," and I believe that he found victory over the prevailing Jewish opinions about Jesus and went on to find saving faith in him.

The point I want to share with you is this: we must never give up on people. Just because a person does not accept Christ the first time he hears about him, does not mean that person is a hopeless case. How many of us would have become Christians if we had had only one chance to say yes to him? We forget that, for most of us, there was a process at work. It took time for us to come around.

This highlights an important principle in our ministry as disciples: we must have persistence in faith and action. This means we must continue to believe that the Word of God, once shared, never lies dormant in the human spirit. It is at work. A person may willfully reject the offers of Christ, but having heard them, he cannot remain ignorant or neutral. Something is going on. This is why we should seed our witnessing with much prayer. After we have had opportunities to share our faith, we should continue to pray for those to whom we have witnessed.

Many examples confirm this truth. A lady recently told me that a relative for whom she had prayed for years had just called to tell her he had become a Christian. My friend was on cloud nine! George Mueller tells the story of a widowed mother who prayed for her lost son each day for over twenty years. She died without seeing his conversion, but he became a Christian the following year. In his testimony he said, "I owe my conversion to the prayers of my mother."

We just do not know in what way God will see fit to touch a life. But we do know that we dare not write off anyone just because he is not interested the first time. There just may be a Nicodemus somewhere waiting to bloom!

Father, I am too much a part of the instant society. I am too indoctrinated with the desire for overnight success and want to see things happen too quickly. Save me from giving up on people because they don't respond the first time. Keep me sensitive and prayerful that they may find you. Amen.

HE'S GONE!

Scripture: John 20:1-2

Text: *We don't know where they have put him! (v. 2).*

Mary lost Jesus and she panicked. She was so sure she knew where he was, but when she returned there, he was gone. Have you ever lost Jesus? Do you know people who have? Can you identify with the feeling of panic at discovering the loss?

This issue is the problem of assumptions and it must be dealt with in discipleship. Mary assumed that Jesus would be where she last saw him, just as we assume Jesus will always be where we left him.

We often assume that Jesus is back in a religious experience of yesterday. It is not uncommon to hear people testify, "I was saved thirty years ago." Great! But what about today? Is your relationship with Christ up-to-date? Many assume that because they had a valid religious experience yesterday, they have Jesus today. The New Testament is clear that salvation is an ongoing process. It has its past dimensions that are essential to the faith, but it also has its present elements and future consequences. Certain experiences in life cause us to reach out for Christ, but when some people do, they cry, "He's gone!" They left him in the yesterdays of their lives and have done very little to cultivate his presence in the now.

Sometimes we assume Jesus is back at the church, and we go there once a week to worship him. In our curious brand of cultural Christianity we have the attitude that we pay our spiritual dues by attending church on Sunday and giving something in the offering. Then, the reasoning goes, we are free to live pretty much as we want for the rest of the week. The problem is that this view of the faith completely overlooks the lordship of Jesus. If he is Lord at all, he is Lord of all—every day's experiences, each moment, all of life. It is only as we begin to discover this that we begin to see the life-style of discipleship. Some people go to church on Sunday and say, "He's gone!" They have tried to leave Jesus at the church, and now they cannot find him even there.

Christ lies dead in our yesterdays, just like he was dead in the tomb. He lies dead if we limit him to the sanctuary, stained glass, and Sunday. Jesus is the Christ of resurrection! Even though men try to put him in tombs of their own making, he rises beyond and above them and moves out into life. He is the Christ of the present. We should not seek him in our yesterdays. He is the Christ of the now. We need to discover him in every dimension of our lives—today. Then we will never have to say, "He's gone!"

Father, help me remember you are not a God to be revered as a museum piece, but a God to be related to—a living Lord. I know you are not back there. You are here. Help me to always seek you. Amen.

TAKING IT ALL IN

Scripture: John 20:3-9

Text: *They still did not understand the Scripture that Jesus had to rise from the dead (v. 9).*

Peter and (probably) John raced to the tomb. Their minds were blown as they found it empty. The text records that the "other disciple" (v. 2, we think it was John) saw the whole thing "and believed" (v. 8). He did not believe anyone had stolen the body; he believed Jesus had risen from the dead. His experience was 100 percent correct, although the very next verse said he still did not understand the Scriptures that taught this.

This raises a question, Is it possible to experience something without understanding the Scripture about it? Some would say no. Some would say that you have to rationalize it out, that you have to intellectualize it as thoroughly as you can. Then when you have it figured out, you can make it a part of your experience. There are those who have become Christians just like that.

But real life also teaches us that there are times when experience precedes understanding. I have talked with many laymen who had read about new birth for years, but never really understood it until it happened to them. They experienced it, then they understood it.

John Wesley was trying to understand faith. He was working to grasp it from an intellectual, performance-oriented point of view. But on the deck of a storm-tossed ship he *saw* faith in some Moravians. It still defied his understanding, but it sparked his curiosity. Later at a meeting, he experienced faith. Then he was able to understand it, articulate it, and spread it across England. For Wesley, experience preceded meaningful understanding.

In your life there will be experiences of God that transcend your understanding. Do not deny them. They are confirmation points along the way to enrich your searching and develop your understanding. It is because I experience God that I want to understand him more and more.

I believe John included this phrase to show us there are times when our experience runs ahead of and feeds our understanding. But I also believe he included it to show us that later on the disciples came to understand the Scriptures as well as to have the experience. Ultimately the two go together, for the life of discipleship is a life of rich experiences. But these experiences should lead us to deeper inquiry and more disciplined searching of the Word so that we may understand and share our experiences of God.

Thank you, Lord, that you are the God of experiences, because they help me know I am not engaged in the pursuit of something dead or obsolete. Thank you that my living experiences challenge me to expand my understanding. Amen.

SEEING JESUS TODAY

Scripture: John 20:10-14

Text: *She . . . saw Jesus . . . but she did not realize that it was Jesus (v. 14).*

We have thought about how Jesus is active *now*. We have seen how he cannot be enshrined in yesterday's religious experience or left at the church, for he has broken out of our yesterdays and our stained glass to move among men and nations of today. The disciple must learn this lesson and see Jesus at work in the world, or he will be like Mary, who saw Jesus but did not realize it was he. I believe Jesus is in many places today, but we do not always recognize that he is there.

First, I believe Jesus is present in today's pressing social problems—world hunger and starvation, abortion, discrimination, poverty, illiteracy, class struggles. You add to the list. This does not mean that we can deify the social problem or equate salvation with social liberation, but it does mean that we acknowledge that the gospel has something to say to people caught up in these problems. Otherwise the Christian faith is irrelevant. The disciple must see Jesus in the social problems of the day and prophetically speak the Word of God to those problems. In some cases, this may mean a proclamation of judgment. In other cases it will mean sharing the good news of love, patience, tolerance, and deliverance. But in all cases it will mean struggling with these problems because we see Jesus there.

Second, Jesus is present in the governments of men. The New Testament speaks of a relationship between human leaders and the providence of God. And we must remember that when it speaks of being "subject to the governing authorities" (Rom. 13:1, RSV), it is speaking about loyalty in the face of a pagan system. God has never abandoned the political arena. We must not either.

Our nation has been founded on the idea of separation of church and state, but that idea was not meant to project an impassable gulf between the two. As one church leader put it, "The ideal recognized the sovereignty of the church, not the state. Its purpose was not to keep the church out of the state, but to prevent the state from abusing the church." Therefore, we should see Jesus in the governments of our day—even the pagan ones. We should be thankful to God for the Christians engaged in politics and diplomacy, and pray that God will send more laborers into this vineyard. We also should pray for those who are already there, that they may live by their convictions and advance the cause of Christ where they serve.

Third, Jesus is present in the masses of lost people. He is more concerned about people than about institutions or systems. Even among systems that are corrupt, dishonest, and cruel, there are still people whose hearts hunger for the Word of God. As disciples, we will pray for divine sensitivity to such people. We will make people our priority because we see Jesus there. This means that evangelism will remain the top priority of the church, because we will labor in the hope that changed lives will result in changed societies. We will cooperate with Christian brothers and sisters all over the world in vigorous and relevant missionary ministries because we see Jesus there.

As we grow in our discipleship, we need to pray to God to increase, expand, and sensitize our vision. Jesus is walking the roads of many lands today. He is present in the needs of many people. See him there. Join him there.

Father, help me to see Jesus wherever he is today. Amen.

BY NAME

Scripture: John 20:15-18

Text: *Jesus said to her, "Mary" (v. 16).*

Christ does not love the world. He loves the people who make up the world—one by one. His love for people is as special as the people themselves, for his relationship with each of us is tailor-made to our individual uniqueness. We must remember this in the life of discipleship.

There was never a more diverse group of people than the first disciples. Among them were fishermen, tax collectors, and political zealots. Yet Jesus had such a unique relationship with each of them that it changed all of their lives.

I can never read this simple verse in John's Gospel without pausing to remember how uniquely I am loved by Christ. Sometimes I am tempted to think that God is busy running the world and therefore not that involved in my life. But that is not so! Jesus knows and relates to us by name.

He calls us by name in salvation. The scriptural requirement is new birth, but talk with born-again Christians and you'll find that no two have had exactly the same experience. They are all born again, but they have come to Christ in unique ways. And the experience itself is unique to their needs—something I must remember in my witnessing. It is the *fact* of salvation, not the *form*, that I am interested in. I know that Christ's salvation will touch people in ways that are special to them, because they are special.

He calls us by name in discipleship and Christian growth. The Scriptures indicate that Christ's call to the first apostles was intensely personal. He did not run a general want ad in the *Jerusalem Herald*. He did not put up posters around town. He went to Simon's and Andrew's boat. He stopped by Matthew's tax office. When he appointed the twelve apostles, "Jesus went up into the hills and called to him those he wanted" (Mark 3:13). The dimension of discipleship was as individual as the people he called.

In Christ's call to discipleship, he equips each of us through the gifts of the Spirit. Every individual is equipped differently, as God sees fit. Thus, we see growing Christians who have a burning zeal for witnessing. Others like to teach. Others want to be sent to places of need. It goes on and on. The individualized discipleship and Christian growth give the church its beauty, variety, strength, and ministry.

He calls us by name in times of crisis. "My grace is sufficient for *you*," he told Paul (II Cor. 12:9). Here is Mary, brokenhearted, afraid. And Jesus comes. He calls her by name. Her spirit is transformed.

In the pastoral ministry I am constantly with people in crisis experiences, and I see the grace of God coming to each person in very special ways. God has no package deals when it comes to his presence and his help. To each and every one he comes in ways that speak to them where they are.

I do not know your need today, but Christ does. Listen, he is calling you by name!

Heavenly Father, you know me by name because you made me. You made me different from any other person who has ever lived or who will ever live. I believe that because I am special, you have a special relationship for me today. Thank you for that. Amen.

PEACE WITH SUBSTANCE

Scripture: John 20:19-29

Text: *"Peace be with you!" After he said this, he showed them his hands and side (vv. 19, 20).*

One of my favorite "Peanuts" comic strips is one in which Snoopy is shivering in the cold. Charlie Brown comes along in the next picture, sees Snoopy, and says, "Snoopy, be warm and filled!" In the final block of the strip, Snoopy is looking in the direction Charlie has gone, and he is still shivering. Words without substance leave us shivering.

This is the way it would have been if Jesus had said "Peace!" when he was invisible. That's the way it would have been if he had been only a ghost. No one is very inspired by hearing voices or seeing ghosts floating around, so John says in two places that after Jesus told them to be at peace, he backed it up with substance.

The first experience was in his declaration on the evening of the first day of the week. After Jesus said, "Peace be with you," he showed them his hands and side. The disciples were overjoyed. Why? Because they had something on which to base their peace.

A week later Jesus showed himself particularly to Thomas. Again, Jesus said, "Peace be with you!" But then he spoke to Thomas, "Put your finger here; see my hands. Reach out your hand and put it into my side" (v. 27). Thomas replied, "My Lord and my God!" (v. 28). Peace with substance.

What does this say to us in our discipleship? It says that in our faith we do not have to act blindly. We do not have to trust in a vacuum. We do not have to try to conjure up any feelings of love, peace, or joy with nothing to go on. The Christian faith is not just floating around with nothing to tie it to. It has substance and confirmation for our Christian experience.

But it also says something to our Christian ministry. It says that we must back up our words with our lives, our actions, and our ministries. Snoopy is still shivering although Charlie has said, "Be warm and filled." People are still left with an empty feeling after hearing us say, "God loves you" if they sense we don't.

Jesus gave substance to his words, and that substance is still real to us in our experience. It must also be present in our service. Otherwise there will be a lot of shivering going on.

Dear God, thank you that I do not have to believe in a vacuum. Thank you for substance. In my service, let me give substance. Do not allow me to ask people to believe only in words. Do not allow me to be concerned only with words. Let me say "Peace," and then give them something of you to bring peace to them. Amen.

WHICH KIND ARE YOU?

Scripture: John 21:1-6

Text: *Throw your net on the right side of the boat and you will find some (v. 6).*

There are only two kinds of life-styles: self-generated or God-generated. Both are portrayed in this section.

First, we see the self-generated life in the disciples' toiling for fish on the Sea of Tiberias. They worked hard all night. They sweat. They pulled on the large nets and dragged them all over the lake. They were professional fishermen who knew how to catch fish, but they caught nothing.

The self-generated life is the life that works on its own ideas and under its own power. There are toil, sweat, and labor, but the end result is nothing substantive for the Kingdom.

I fear we operate this way in the church sometimes. We form committees, make elaborate plans, and call in the experts to help us plan our programs. We work and sweat, but we come up with empty nets. Something is wrong.

Vance Havner in his book *The Secret of Christian Joy* compares this self-generated labor to workmen in a logging camp: "Many of the Lord's workmen have lost the axe head of power. The workmen are chopping with the handle." Much of our time is spent beating on trees with bare handles because we are living self-generated lives. But then Jesus speaks, and everything changes. The nets that were empty are now full to the tearing point. They are brimming with fish.

Notice that the fish did not appear magically. The disciples had to throw the nets in again. They had to work, but now it was labor with a purpose because they had divine direction. The work made sense, and it paid off.

I am not advocating a discipleship that says, "It's the Lord's Kingdom; he will bring it in." I am not advocating a view of Christianity that looks heavenward all the time waiting for the

Second Coming. Rather, I am pleading for a discipleship that gets its marching orders before it marches. I am calling for a life-style that seeks God's will first, then works in the light of that will. I am praying for a church that first struggles with God's will and then plans for ministry in accord with that will.

It is only a slight change, but it makes all the difference. If we persist in toiling without first hearing the word of the master, we will keep pulling empty nets. But if we will live God-generated lives, our work in his name will pull in a hearty catch for the Kingdom.

I have to keep checking myself at this point. Too often I am self-generated. Too often I decide to go fishing, get my nets all set, and then ask God to bless what I'm doing. Instead, he is calling me to heed his direction. Then he can use my nets, and I will know any glory is all because of him.

Father, too often I try to work in the energy of my own ideas and strength. Slow me down, Lord, and make me realize that first I must get your directions. Then I can follow them productively. Amen.

THE ETERNAL PROVIDER

Scripture John 21:7-14

Text: *Jesus came, took the bread and gave it to them, and did the same with the fish (v. 13).*

John 21 tells of a transition period. Jesus was nearing the end of his earthly ministry and approaching the time when he would be our shepherd through the Spirit.

Jesus gave specific instructions to the disciples about their fishing. But in doing so he was reminding them that he would guide them eternally and would make their labors fruitful eternally. Men motivated by the master will always have full nets.

In this section John tells how Jesus built a fire and cooked breakfast for the disciples. He served them bread and fish. That is the historical situation. But the spiritual reality is that Jesus provides for our needs and satisfies our hunger. What he was doing for the disciples on that early morning, he would do for them eternally.

Oral Roberts has rendered Christianity a great service by reminding us that God is our source. He keeps holding before us this verse: "My God will meet all your needs according to his glorious riches in Christ Jesus" (Phil. 4:19).

We need to remember that in our discipleship. We are blessed as no other generation has been in our multitude of spiritual resources to help us grow. There are many gifted teachers across the nation imparting spiritual food. There are television and radio programs. There are books, movies, video and cassette tapes. We should praise God that we have so many aids to Christian growth, but we dare not fall prey to desiring these things more than the master himself. Some of us seem more excited about getting the next spiritual nugget from our earthly shepherds than in feeding on the words of the eternal shepherd. Others among us are more excited about hearing the next message from the well-known pastor so-and-so than in spending quiet moments at home with God.

Our argument is, "But God uses these things to bless me." Fine! As long as we remember to keep that perspective. Such resources will feed us as long as we regard them properly as instruments in the hands of the eternal provider, but they will poison us when we become more interested in the men than in the message.

I fought this in the early part of my Christian life and in the first days of my ministry. I practically worshiped Billy Graham, reading everything he wrote and incorporating much of his material in my sermons. I think I even unconsciously tried to style my delivery after his. But one day all that had to stop for I was shown very clearly that the greatness of Billy Graham was due to his source not to himself. I discovered that any spiritual greatness I might ever attain would not come from being like anyone else, but in being a Christian. So I let go of Billy and took hold of the master. I still appreciate and follow Billy Graham's ministry, but for an entirely different reason.

Remember, there is a fire in our lives. It has some bread and fish on it for our nourishment. The bread and fish are great to feed on and the fire is warm, but none of it would be there if it were not for Jesus, the eternal provider.

Father, thank you for the many avenues of growth you have provided for me today. Help me use them as tools, not follow them as masters. I acknowledge that you are my one and only source. Amen.

THE INDISPENSABLE QUALITY

Scripture: John 21:15-19

Text: *Simon son of John, do you truly love me . . . ? (v. 15).*

This significant section has been debated by the best scholars. You might find it interesting to examine it in detail with the help of commentaries. As before, we are confronted with the historical fact and the spiritual significance. Jesus was searching out the love of Peter, but the reason lay far beyond the immediate situation.

Jesus was looking forward to the time when Peter would bear important leadership responsibilities. He was looking back to the time at Caesarea Philippi when Peter first declared Jesus to be the Christ, and when Jesus promised that it would be on such a foundation of truth that the church would be built.

First, Jesus sought to determine the love of Peter. Did Peter really love the master? Just recently he seemed willing to leave everything and go fishing. Was Christ still the top priority of his life? I believe Jesus was conscious that only a few days earlier Peter had flatly denied any relationship with him, and now he needed to know where Peter stood. Did he love him? So Jesus asked him three times, both to parallel Peter's three denials, and also, I think, for the dramatic effect. John says that when Jesus asked the third time, it hurt Peter. The importance of the situation is driven home in the threefold repetition. Personally, I do not see any major significance to the changes of use in the Greek for the word *love*, although some scholars do. Rather, I see Jesus seeking to sound the depths of that love to make sure it is real.

How often Christ has to ask me, "Do you love me?" On the surface I can give a quick answer, "Sure, you know I do."

Then he asks again, a little deeper, beginning to pull the cover off my attitudes, my inconsistencies, my compromises. "Do you really love me?"

I reply, "Yes, Lord, I love you despite my imperfections."

Then he asks again. And this time I am moved to repentance and recommitment. After he nails it down one more time, he moves on. Jesus had to do this with Peter.

But he also had to teach Peter the indispensable quality of love. If Peter was going to be a leader in the church, one quality would have to stand out above all others—love. This love would have to express itself in action: feeding, caring, tending. Again, some scholars have tried to make an issue of Jesus' three requests, but I do not see that as the main point. Instead, I see the emphasis on expressing that love through ministry and service. Jesus was calling for a leadership lived out in love.

He calls upon us for the same thing. He wants us to do more than sing, "Oh, how I love Jesus." He wants us to love—in action. Today, as then, love is the indispensable quality. After Jesus finds out whether we really have love or not, he will let us know that we have to put it to work. Only then will we be ready to lead.

Thank you, God, that you keep asking, "Do you love me?" Thank you that you will not let me get away with surface answers and love in word only. Amen.

I WANT YOU!

Scripture: John 21:20-25

Text: *Lord, what about him? (v. 21).*

It is a strange characteristic of human nature to wonder about other people. Gossip thrives on this. Millions of newspapers and magazines give us the scoop on other people. For some reason Peter wanted to know about John. We don't know the real reason, but I've always felt that Peter really wanted to change the subject. He had just been interrogated pretty heavily, and now he wanted to move on to some other topic. Yet, the answer Jesus gave Peter provides insight into the nature of our discipleship.

First, Jesus was telling Peter that he had a personal plan for each of them. What he willed for John was not to be Peter's main concern. Peter's first task was to discover, accept, and live out the plan Jesus had for him.

We are to serve where we are put. We are not to wonder why another person is doing this or that; we are only to be concerned with whether or not we are serving God faithfully where we are.

Often people complain that someone else got the job they deserved, and their jealousy makes them less effective where they are. Some preachers secretly envy their brothers for getting the appointments that they wanted themselves, and their jealousy weakens their service where they are. The saying "Bloom where you are planted" is appropriate here. We are not to be concerned about God's plan for others' lives; we are just to be faithful where we are.

Second, Jesus is telling Peter that we never find glory in comparing ourselves with others, but rather in the faithfulness we exhibit in serving Christ in the way he has shown us.

I struggled with this right after my first book was published. When I saw my name in print like other authors I had admired,

I falsely compared myself with them and tried to find some new glory in being an author too. But the Lord told me, "Steve, any glory you receive from that book is only because you were faithful in writing what you felt I wanted you to write." So I still am not like any other author, book or no book, for I only did what I felt God compelled me to do. We only receive true glory when we are faithful to what God is calling us to do.

This is not a case for self-centeredness but simply a statement that as disciples we are to be faithful to God's plan for us. If we do that, we can be sure Jesus will accomplish his plan for other disciples too.

Lord Jesus, you've made me special, and yet I waste too much time trying to be like other people. I spend too much time wondering what you are doing with them, and not enough time letting you work in me. Help me surrender to your uniqueness for me. Amen.

WE'VE ONLY JUST BEGUN

Scripture: John 20:30-31

Text: *That by believing you may have life in his name (v. 31).*

Today is our last day together. I thought it would be fitting for us to end at the point we began nearly three months ago. I have shared how this verse is the window for the whole Gospel, for belief in Jesus gives life.

As we wind things up, let's change the image just a bit and say, first of all, that my purpose in sharing with you each day has been to strengthen your belief in Jesus. I have tried to present John's Gospel in such a way as to cause you to reflect on your own relationship with Christ. If I have done this, then our time together has been fruitful.

I hope I have shown how multifaceted our belief is, how it applies in so many areas. If I have helped you to expand your understanding of discipleship, then our time together has been helpful.

But in the final analysis my purpose is just like John puts it: "that by believing you may have life in his name." Life is what it is all about! The Christian faith is not a creed to be professed; it is a life to be lived—the most abundant life to be found anywhere! It is the kind of life that cannot be quenched at death; rather it lives on for eternity. This life that is found in a relationship with God through Jesus Christ. If you have begun to live more in these past three months, then my prayers for this book have been answered.

I am confident that in the coming days you will return to the Gospel of John many times, and you will probably want to plow through on increasingly deeper levels. Here are a few resources I hope you will have in your library as you return to John in the future:

Barclay, William. *The Daily Study Bible*. Philadelphia: Westminster Press, 1977.

Blaney, Harvey. "John." In *The Wesleyan Bible Commentary*. Grand Rapids: Wm. B. Eerdmans, 1964. Vol. 4: *Matthew–Acts*.

Boice, James Montgomery. *The Gospel of John*. Grand Rapids: Zondervan, 1978. A five-volume expositional commentary.

Morris, Leon. *The Gospel According to John*. In the New International Commentary on the New Testament. Grand Rapids: Wm. B. Eerdmans, 1970.

Tasker, R.V.G. *John*. In the Tyndale New Testament Commentaries. Grand Rapids: Wm. B. Eerdmans, 1960.

I am confident these volumes will help you in further study of this rich Bible book.

As we close, what I really want to do is pray with you. Go where you can be quiet and comfortable, and enter into this prayer as if we were actually together. I want this to be for *you!*

Heavenly Father, thank you that you have allowed us to spend these days together. Thank you that by your providence you allowed me to write this book and that you led my friend to use it. My deepest hope is that it may have been a fruitful experience for both of us. We are fellow strugglers in the life of discipleship, fellow pilgrims in search of more meaningful faith. Let your Spirit fill us now. Let us hear the call of discipleship more clearly and respond with more dedication and enthusiasm than ever before. Thank you, God, for giving us a fresh start! In the master's name we pray. Amen.